6. Enter your class ID code to join a class.

IF YOU HAVE A CLASS CODE FROM YOUR TEACHER

a. Enter your class code and click [Next]

b. Once you have joined a class, you will be able to use the Discussion Board and Email tools.

c. To enter this code later, choose **Join a Class**.

IF YOU DO NOT HAVE A CLASS CODE

a. If you do not have a class ID code, click [Skip]

b. You do not need a class ID code to use *iQ Online*.

c. To enter this code later, choose **Join a Class**.

7. Review registration information and click Log In. Then choose your book. Click **Activities** to begin using *iQ Online*.

IMPORTANT

- After you register, the next time you want to use *iQ Online*, go to www.iQOnlinePractice.com and log in with your email address and password.
- The online content can be used for 12 months from the date you register.
- For help, please contact customer service: eltsupport@oup.com.

WHAT IS iQ ONLINE ?

All new activities provide essential skills **practice** and support.

Vocabulary and Grammar **games** immerse you in the language and provide even more practice.

Authentic, engaging **videos** generate new ideas and opinions on the Unit Question.

Go to the Media Center to download or stream all **student book audio**.

Use the **Discussion Board** to discuss the Unit Question and more.

Email encourages communication with your teacher and classmates.

Automatic grading gives immediate feedback and tracks progress.

Progress Reports show what you have mastered and where you still need more practice.

SHAPING learning TOGETHER

We would like to acknowledge the teachers from all over the world who participated in the development process and review of the Q series.

Special thanks to our Q: Skills for Success Second Edition Topic Advisory Board

Shaker Ali Al-Mohammad, Buraimi University College, Oman; **Dr. Asmaa A. Ebrahim**, University of Sharjah, U.A.E.; **Rachel Batchilder**, College of the North Atlantic, Qatar; **Anil Bayir**, Izmir University, Turkey; **Flora Mcvay Bozkurt**, Maltepe University, Turkey; **Paul Bradley**, University of the Thai Chamber of Commerce Bangkok, Thailand; **Joan Birrell-Bertrand**, University of Manitoba, MB, Canada; **Karen E. Caldwell**, Zayed University, U.A.E.; **Nicole Hammond Carrasquel**, University of Central Florida, FL, U.S.; **Kevin Countryman**, Seneca College of Applied Arts & Technology, ON, Canada; **Julie Crocker**, Arcadia University, NS, Canada; **Marc L. Cummings**, Jefferson Community and Technical College, KY, U.S.; **Rachel DeSanto**, Hillsborough Community College Dale Mabry Campus, FL, U.S.; **Nilüfer Ertürkmen**, Ege University, Turkey; **Sue Fine**, Ras Al Khaimah Women's College (HCT), U.A.E.; **Amina Al Hashami**, Nizwa College of Applied Sciences, Oman; **Stephan Johnson**, Nagoya Shoka Daigaku, Japan; **Sean Kim**, Avalon, South Korea; **Gregory King**, Chubu Daigaku, Japan; **Seran Küçük**, Maltepe University, Turkey; **Jonee De Leon**, VUS, Vietnam; **Carol Lowther**, Palomar College, CA, U.S.; **Erin Harris-MacLeod**, St. Mary's University, NS, Canada; **Angela Nagy**, Maltepe University, Turkey; **Huynh Thi Ai Nguyen**, Vietnam; **Daniel L. Paller**, Kinjo Gakuin University, Japan; **Jangyo Parsons**, Kookmin University, South Korea; **Laila Al Qadhi**, Kuwait University, Kuwait; **Josh Rosenberger**, English Language Institute University of Montana, MT, U.S.; **Nancy Schoenfeld**, Kuwait University, Kuwait; **Jenay Seymour**, Hongik University, South Korea; **Moon-young Son**, South Korea; **Matthew Taylor**, Kinjo Gakuin Daigaku, Japan; **Burcu Tezcan-Unal**, Zayed University, U.A.E.; **Troy Tucker**, Edison State College-Lee Campus, FL, U.S.; **Kris Vicca**, Feng Chia University, Taichung; **Jisook Woo**, Incheon University, South Korea; **Dunya Yenidunya**, Ege University, Turkey

UNITED STATES Marcarena Aguilar, North Harris College, TX; Rebecca Andrade, California State University North Ridge, CA; Lesley Andrews, Boston University, MA; Deborah Anholt, Lewis and Clark College, OR; Robert Anzelde, Oakton Community College, IL; Arlys Arnold, University of Minnesota, MN; Marcia Arthur, Renton Technical College, WA; Renee Ashmeade, Passaic County Community College, NJ; Anne Bachmann, Clackamas Community College, OR; Lida Baker, UCLA, CA; Ron Balsamo, Santa Rosa Junior College, CA; Lori Barkley, Portland State University, OR; Eileen Barlow, SUNY Albany, NY; Sue Bartch, Cuyahoga Community College, OH; Lora Bates, Oakton High School, VA; Barbara Batra, Nassau County Community College, NY; Nancy Baum, University of Texas at Arlington, TX; Rebecca Beck, Irvine Valley College, CA; Linda Berendsen, Oakton Community College, IL; Jennifer Binckes Lee, Howard Community College, MD; Grace Bishop, Houston Community College, TX; Jean W. Bodman, Union County College, NJ; Virginia Bouchard, George Mason University, VA; Kimberley Briesch Sumner, University of Southern California, CA; Kevin Brown, University of California, Irvine, CA; Laura Brown, Glendale Community College, CA; Britta Burton, Mission College, CA; Allison L. Callahan, Harold Washington College, IL; Gabriela Cambiasso, Harold Washington College, IL; Jackie Campbell, Capistrano Unified School District, CA; Adele C. Camus, George Mason University, VA; Laura Chason, Savannah College, GA; Kerry Linder Catana, Language Studies International, NY; An Cheng, Oklahoma State University, OK; Carole Collins, North Hampton Community College, PA; Betty R. Compton, Intercultural Communications College, HI; Pamela Couch, Boston University, MA; Fernanda Crowe, Intrax International Institute, CA; Vicki Curtis, Santa Cruz, CA; Margo Czinski, Washtenaw Community College, MI; David Dahnke, Lone Star College, TX; Gillian M. Dale, CA; L. Dalgish, Concordia College, MN; Christopher Davis, John Jay College, NY; Sherry Davis, Irvine University, CA; Natalia de Cuba, Nassau County Community College, NY; Sonia Delgadillo, Sierra College, CA; Esmeralda Diriye, Cypress College & Cal Poly, CA; Marta O. Dmytrenko-Ahrabian, Wayne State University, MI; Javier Dominguez, Central High School, SC; Jo Ellen Downey-Greer, Lansing Community College, MI; Jennifer Duclos, Boston University, MA; Yvonne Duncan, City College of San Francisco, CA; Paul Dydman, USC Language Academy, CA; Anna Eddy, University of Michigan-Flint, MI; Zohan El-Gamal, Glendale Community College, CA; Jennie Farnell, University of Connecticut, CT; Susan Fedors, Howard Community College, MD; Valerie Fiechter, Mission College, CA; Ashley Fifer, Nassau County Community College, NY; Matthew Florence, Intrax International Institute, CA; Kathleen Flynn, Glendale College, CA; Elizabeth Fonsea, Nassau County Community College, NY; Eve Fonseca, St. Louis Community College, MO; Elizabeth Foss, Washtenaw Community College, MI; Duff C. Galda, Pima Community College, AZ; Christiane Galvani, Houston Community College, TX; Gretchen Gerber, Howard Community College, MD; Ray Gonzalez, Montgomery College, MD; Janet Goodwin, University of California, Los Angeles, CA; Alyona Gorokhova, Grossmont College, CA; John Graney, Santa Fe College, FL; Kathleen Green, Central High School, AZ; Nancy Hamadou, Pima Community College-West Campus, AZ; Webb Hamilton, De Anza College, San Jose City College, CA; Janet Harclerode, Santa Monica Community College, CA; Sandra Hartmann, Language and Culture Center, TX; Kathy Haven, Mission College, CA; Roberta Hendrick, Cuyahoga Community College, OH; Ginny Heringer, Pasadena City College, CA; Adam Henricksen, University of Maryland, MD; Carolyn Ho, Lone Star College-CyFair, TX; Peter Hoffman, LaGuardia Community College, NY; Linda Holden, College of Lake County, IL; Jana Holt, Lake Washington Technical College, WA; Antonio Iccarino, Boston University, MA; Gail Ibele, University of Wisconsin, WI; Nina Ito, American Language Institute, CSU Long Beach, CA; Linda Jensen, UCLA, CA; Lisa Jurkowitz, Pima Community College, CA; Mandy Kama, Georgetown University, Washington, DC; Stephanie Kasuboski, Cuyahoga Community College, OH; Chigusa Katoku, Mission College, CA; Sandra Kawamura, Sacramento City College, CA; Gail Kellersberger, University of Houston-Downtown, TX; Jane Kelly, Durham Technical Community College, NC; Maryanne Kildare, Nassau County Community College, NY; Julie Park Kim, George Mason University, VA; Kindra Kinyon, Los Angeles Trade-Technical College, CA; Matt Kline, El Camino College, CA; Lisa Kovacs-Morgan, University of California, San Diego, CA; Claudia Kupiec, DePaul University, IL; Renee La Rue, Lone Star College-Montgomery, TX; Janet Langon, Glendale College, CA; Lawrence Lawson, Palomar College, CA; Rachele Lawton, The Community College of Baltimore County, MD; Alice Lee, Richland College, TX; Esther S. Lee, CSUF & Mt. SAC, CA; Cherie Lenz-Hackett, University of Washington, WA; Joy Leventhal, Cuyahoga Community College, OH; Alice Lin, UCI Extension, CA; Monica Lopez, Cerritos College, CA; Dustin Lovell, FLS International Marymount College, CA; Carol Lowther, Palomar College, CA; Candace Lynch-Thompson, North Orange County Community College District, CA; Thi Thi Ma, City College of San Francisco, CA; Steve Mac Isaac, USC Long Academy, CA; Denise Maduli-Williams, City College of San Francisco, CA; Eileen Mahoney, Camelback High School, AZ; Naomi Mardock, MCC-Omaha, NE; Brigitte Maronde, Harold Washington College, IL; Marilyn Marquis, Laposita College CA; Doris Martin, Glendale Community College; Pasadena City College, CA; Keith Maurice, University of Texas at Arlington, TX; Nancy Mayer, University of Missouri-St. Louis, MO; Aziah McNamara, Kansas State University, KS; Billie McQuillan, Education Heights, MN; Karen Merritt, Glendale Union High School District, AZ; Holly Milkowart, Johnson County Community College, KS; Eric Moyer, Intrax International Institute, CA; Gino Muzzatti, Santa Rosa Junior College, CA; Sandra Navarro, Glendale Community College, CA; Than Nyeinkhin, ELAC, PCC, CA; William Nedrow, Triton College, IL; Eric Nelson, University of Minnesota, MN; Than Nyeinkhin, ELAC, PCC, CA; Fernanda Ortiz, Center for English as a Second Language at the University of Arizona, AZ; Rhony Ory, Ygnacio Valley High School, CA; Paul Parent, Montgomery College, MD; Dr. Sumeeta Patnaik, Marshall University, WV; Oscar Pedroso, Miami Dade College, FL; Robin Persiani, Sierra College, CA; Patricia Prenz-Belkin, Hostos Community College, NY; Suzanne Powell, University of Louisville, KY; Jim Ranalli, Iowa State University, IA; Toni R. Randall, Santa Monica College, CA; Vidya Rangachari, Mission College, CA; Elizabeth Rasmussen, Northern Virginia Community College, VA; Lara Ravitch, Truman College, IL;

Deborah Repasz, San Jacinto College, TX; **Marisa Recinos**, English Language Center, Brigham Young University, UT; **Andrey Reznikov**, Black Hills State University, SD; **Alison Rice**, Hunter College, NY; **Jennifer Robles**, Ventura Unified School District, CA; **Priscilla Rocha**, Clark County School District, NV; **Dzidra Rodins**, DePaul University, IL; **Maria Rodriguez**, Central High School, AZ; **Josh Rosenberger**, English Language Institute University of Montana, MT; **Alice Rosso**, Bucks County Community College, PA; **Rita Rozzi**, Xavier University, OH; **Maria Ruiz**, Victor Valley College, CA; **Kimberly Russell**, Clark College, WA; **Stacy Sabraw**, Michigan State University, MI; **Irene Sakk**, Northwestern University, IL; **Deborah Sandstrom**, University of Illinois at Chicago, IL; **Jenni Santamaria**, ABC Adult, CA; **Shaeley Santiago**, Ames High School, IA; **Peg Sarosy**, San Francisco State University, CA; **Alice Savage**, North Harris College, TX; **Donna Schaeffer**, University of Washington, WA; **Karen Marsh Schaeffer**, University of Utah, UT; **Carol Schinger**, Northern Virginia Community College, VA; **Robert Scott**, Kansas State University, KS; **Suell Scott**, Sheridan Technical Center, FL; **Shira Seaman**, Global English Academy, NY; **Richard Seltzer**, Glendale Community College, CA; **Harlan Sexton**, CUNY Queensborough Community College, NY; **Kathy Sherak**, San Francisco State University, CA; **German Silva**, Miami Dade College, FL; **Ray Smith**, Maryland English Institute, University of Maryland, MD; **Shira Smith**, NICE Program University of Hawaii, HI; **Tara Smith**, Felician College, NJ; **Monica Snow**, California State University, Fullerton, CA; **Elaine Soffer**, Nassau County Community College, NY; **Andrea Spector**, Santa Monica Community College, CA; **Jacqueline Sport**, LBWCC Luverne Center, AL; **Karen Stanely**, Central Piedmont Community College, NC; **Susan Stern**, Irvine Valley College, CA; **Ayse Stromsdorfer**, Soldan I.S.H.S., MO; **Yilin Sun**, South Seattle Community College, WA; **Thomas Swietlik**, Intrax International Institute, IL; **Nicholas Taggert**, University of Dayton, OH; **Judith Tanka**, UCLA Extension–American Language Center, CA; **Amy Taylor**, The University of Alabama Tuscaloosa, AL; **Andrea Taylor**, San Francisco State, CA; **Priscilla Taylor**, University of Southern California, CA; **Ilene Teixeira**, Fairfax County Public Schools, VA; **Shirl H. Terrell**, Collin College, TX; **Marya Teutsch-Dwyer**, St. Cloud State University, MN; **Stephen Thergesen**, ELS Language Centers, CO; **Christine Tierney**, Houston Community College, TX; **Arlene Turini**, North Moore High School, NC; **Cara Tuzzolino**, Nassau County Community College, NY; **Suzanne Van Der Valk**, Iowa State University, IA; **Nathan D. Vasarhely**, Ygnacio Valley High School, CA; **Naomi S. Verratti**, Howard Community College, MD; **Hollyahna Vettori**, Santa Rosa Junior College, CA; **Julie Vorholt**, Lewis & Clark College, OR; **Danielle Wagner**, FLS International Marymount College, CA; **Lynn Walker**, Coastline College, CA; **Laura Walsh**, City College of San Francisco, CA; **Andrew J. Watson**, The English Bakery; **Donald Weasenforth**, Collin College, TX; **Juliane Widner**, Sheepshead Bay High School, NY; **Lynne Wilkins**, Mills College, CA; **Pamela Williams**, Ventura College, CA; **Jeff Wilson**, Irvine Valley College, CA; **James Wilson**, Consomnes River College, CA; **Katie Windahl**, Cuyahoga Community College, OH; **Dolores "Lorrie" Winter**, California State University at Fullerton, CA; **Jody Yamamoto**, Kapi'olani Community College, HI; **Ellen L. Yaniv**, Boston University, MA; **Norman Yoshida**, Lewis & Clark College, OR; **Joanna Zadra**, American River College, CA; **Florence Zysman**, Santiago Canyon College, CA;

`CANADA` **Patricia Birch**, Brandon University, MB; **Jolanta Caputa**, College of New Caledonia, BC; **Katherine Coburn**, UBC's ELI, BC; **Erin Harris-Macleod**, St. Mary's University, NS; **Tami Moffatt**, English Language Institute, BC; **Jim Papple**, Brock University, ON; **Robin Peace**, Confederation College, BC;

`ASIA` **Rabiatu Abubakar**, Eton Language Centre, Malaysia; **Wiwik Andreani**, Bina Nusantara University, Indonesia; **Frank Bailey**, Baiko Gakuin University, Japan; **Mike Baker**, Kosei Junior High School, Japan; **Leonard Barrow**, Kanto Junior College, Japan; **Herman Bartelen**, Japan; **Siren Betty**, Fooyin University, Kaohsiung; **Thomas E. Bieri**, Nagoya College, Japan; **Natalie Brezden**, Global English House, Japan; **MK Brooks**, Mukogawa Women's University, Japan; **Truong Ngoc Buu**, The Youth Language School, Vietnam; **Charles Cabell**, Toyo University, Japan; **Fred Carruth**, Matsumoto University, Japan; **Frances Causer**, Seijo University, Japan; **Jeffrey Chalk**, SNU, South Korea; **Deborah Chang**, Wenzao Ursuline College of Languages, Kaohsiung; **David Chatham**, Ritsumeikan University, Japan; **Andrew Chih Hong Chen**, National Sun Yat-sen University, Kaohsiung; **Christina Chen**, Yu-Tsai Bilingual Elementary School, Taipei; **Hui-chen Chen**, Shi-Lin High School of Commerce, Taipei; **Seungmoon Choe**, K2M Language Institute, South Korea; **Jason Jeffree Cole**, Coto College, Japan; **Le Minh Cong**, Vungtau Tourism Vocational College, Vietnam; **Todd Cooper**, Toyama National College of Technology, Japan; **Marie Cosgrove**, Daito Bunka

University, Japan; **Randall Cotten**, Gifu City Women's College, Japan; **Tony Cripps**, Ritsumeikan University, Japan; **Andy Cubalit**, CHS, Thailand; **Daniel Cussen**, Takushoku University, Japan; **Le Dan**, Ho Chi Minh City Electric Power College, Vietnam; **Simon Daykin**, Banghwa-dong Community Centre, South Korea; **Aimee Denham**, ILA, Vietnam; **Bryan Dickson**, David's English Center, Taipei; **Nathan Ducker**, Japan University, Japan; **Ian Duncan**, Simul International Corporate Training, Japan; **Nguyen Thi Kieu Dung**, Thang Long University, Vietnam; **Truong Quang Dung**, Tien Giang University, Vietnam; **Nguyen Thi Thuy Duong**, Vietnamese American Vocational Training College, Vietnam; **Wong Tuck Ee**, Raja Tun Azlan Science Secondary School, Malaysia; **Emilia Effendy**, International Islamic University Malaysia, Malaysia; **Bettizza Escueta**, KMUTT, Thailand; **Robert Eva**, Kaisei Girls High School, Japan; **Jim George**, Luna International Language School, Japan; **Jurgen Germeys**, Silk Road Language Center, South Korea; **Wong Ai Gnoh**, SMJK Chung Hwa Confucian, Malaysia; **Sarah Go**, Seoul Women's University, South Korea; **Peter Goosselink**, Hokkai High School, Japan; **Robert Gorden**, SNU, South Korea; **Wendy M. Gough**, St. Mary College/Nunoike Gaigo Senmon Gakko, Japan; **Tim Grose**, Sapporo Gakuin University, Japan; **Pham Thu Ha**, Le Van Tam Primary School, Vietnam; **Ann-Marie Hadzima**, Taipei; **Troy Hammond**, Tokyo Gakugei University International Secondary School, Japan; **Robiatul 'Adawiah Binti Hamzah**, SMK Putrajaya Precinct 8(1), Malaysia; **Tran Thi Thuy Hang**, Ho Chi Minh City Banking University, Vietnam; **To Thi Hong Hanh**, CEFALT, Vietnam; **George Hays**, Tokyo Kokusai Daigaku, Japan; **Janis Hearn**, Hongik University, South Korea; **Chantel Hemmi**, Jochi Daigaku, Japan; **David Hindman**, Sejong University, South Korea; **Nahn Cam Hoa**, Ho Chi Minh City University of Technology, Vietnam; **Jana Holt**, Korea University, South Korea; **Jason Hollowell**, Nihon University, Japan; **F. N. (Zoe) Hsu**, National Tainan University, Yong Kang; **Kuei-ping Hsu**, National Tsing Hua University, Hsinchu City; **Wenhua Hsu**, I-Shou University, Kaohsiung; **Luu Nguyen Quoc Hung**, Cantho University, Vietnam; **Cecile Hwang**, Changwon National University, South Korea; **Ainol Haryati Ibrahim**, Universiti Malaysia Pahang, Malaysia; **Robert Jeens**, Yonsei University, South Korea; **Linda M. Joyce**, Kyushu Sangyo University, Japan; **Dr. Nisai Kaewsanchai**, English Square Kanchanaburi, Thailand; **Aniza Kamarulzaman**, Sabah Science Secondary School, Malaysia; **Ikuko Kashiwabara**, Osaka Electro-Communication University, Japan; **Gurmit Kaur**, INTI College, Malaysia; **Nick Keane**, Japan; **Ward Ketcheson**, Aomori University, Japan; **Nicholas Kemp**, Kyushu International University, Japan; **Montchatry Ketmuni**, Rajamangala University of Technology, Thailand; **Dinh Viet Khanh**, Vietnam; **Seonok Kim**, Kangsu Jongro Language School, South Korea; **Suyeon Kim**, Anyang University, South Korea; **Kelly P. Kimura**, Soka University, Japan; **Masakazu Kimura**, Katoh Gakuen Gyoshu High School, Japan; **Gregory King**, Chubu Daigaku, Japan; **Stan Kirk**, Konan University, Japan; **Donald Knight**, Nan Hua/Fu Li Junior High Schools, Hsinchu; **Kari J. Kostiainen**, Nagoya City University, Japan; **Pattri Kuanpulpol**, Silpakorn University, Thailand; **Ha Thi Lan**, Thai Binh Teacher Training College, Vietnam; **Eric Edwin Larson**, Miyazaki Prefectural Nursing University, Japan; **David Laurence**, Chubu Daigaku, Japan; **Richard S. Lavin**, Prefectural University of Kumamoto, Japan; **Shirley Leane**, Chugoku Junior College, Japan; **I-Hsiu Lee**, Yunlin; **Nari Lee**, Park Jung PLS, South Korea; **Tae Lee**, Yonsei University, South Korea; **Lys Yongsoon Lee**, Reading Town Geumcheon, South Korea; **Mallory Leece**, Sun Moon University, South Korea; **Dang Hong Lien**, Tan Lam Upper Secondary School, Vietnam; **Huang Li-Han**, Rebecca Education Institute, Taipei; **Sovannarith Lim**, Royal University of Phnom Penh, Cambodia; **Ginger Lin**, National Kaohsiung Hospitality College, Kaohsiung; **Noel Lineker**, New Zealand/Japan; **Tran Dang Khanh Linh**, Nha Trang Teachers' Training College, Vietnam; **Daphne Liu**, Buliton English School, Taipei; **S. F. Josephine Liu**, Tien-Mu Elementary School, Taipei ; **Caroline Luo**, Tunghai University, Taichung; **Jeng-Jia Luo**, Tunghai University, Taichung; **Laura MacGregor**, Gakushuin University, Japan; **Amir Madani**, Visuttharangsi School, Thailand; **Elena Maeda**, Sacred Heart Professional Training College, Japan; **Vu Thi Thanh Mai**, Hoang Gia Education Center, Vietnam; **Kimura Masakazu**, Kato Gakuen Gyoshu High School, Japan; **Susumu Matsuhashi**, Net Link English School, Japan; **James McCrostie**, Daito Bunka University, Japan; **Joel McKee**, Inha University, South Korea; **Colin McKenzie**, Wachirawit Primary School, Thailand; **Terumi Miyazoe**, Tokyo Denki Daigaku, Japan; **William K. Moore**, Hiroshima Kokusai Gakuin University, Japan; **Kevin Mueller**, Tokyo Kokusai Daigaku, Japan; **Hudson Murrell**, Baiko Gakuin University, Japan; **Frances Namba**, Senri International School of Kwansei Gakuin, Japan; **Keiichi Narita**, Niigata University, Japan; **Kim Chung Nguyen**, Ho Chi Minh University of

Industry, Vietnam; **Do Thi Thanh Nhan**, Hanoi University, Vietnam; **Dale Kazuo Nishi**, Aoyama English Conversation School, Japan; **Huynh Thi Ai Nguyen**, Vietnam; **Dongshin Oh**, YBM PLS, South Korea; **Keiko Okada**, Dokkyo Daigaku, Japan; **Louise Ohashi**, Shukutoku University, Japan; **Yongjun Park**, Sangji University, South Korea; **Donald Patnaude**, Ajarn Donald's English Language Services, Thailand; **Virginia Peng**, Ritsumeikan University, Japan; **Suangkanok Piboonthamnont**, Rajamangala University of Technology, Thailand; **Simon Pitcher**, Business English Teaching Services, Japan; **John C. Probert**, New Education Worldwide, Thailand; **Do Thi Hoa Quyen**, Ton Duc Thang University, Vietnam; **John P. Racine**, Dokkyo University, Japan; **Kevin Ramsden**, Kyoto University of Foreign Studies, Japan; **Luis Rappaport**, Cung Thieu Nha Ha Noi, Vietnam; **Lisa Reshad**, Konan Daigaku Hyogo, Japan; **Peter Riley**, Taisho University, Japan; **Thomas N. Robb**, Kyoto Sangyo University, Japan; **Rory Rosszell**, Meiji Daigaku, Japan; **Maria Feti Rosyani**, Universitas Kristen Indonesia, Indonesia; **Greg Rouault**, Konan University, Japan; **Chris Ruddenklau**, Kindai University, Japan; **Hans-Gustav Schwartz**, Thailand; **Mary-Jane Scott**, Soongsil University, South Korea; **Dara Sheahan**, Seoul National University, South Korea; **James Sherlock**, A.P.W. Angthong, Thailand; **Prof. Shieh**, Minghsin University of Science & Technology, Xinfeng; **Yuko Shimizu**, Ritsumeikan University, Japan; **Suzila Mohd Shukor**, Universiti Sains Malaysia, Malaysia; **Stephen E. Smith**, Mahidol University, Thailand; **Moon-young Son**, South Korea; **Seunghee Son**, Anyang University, South Korea; **Mi-young Song**, Kyungwon University, South Korea; **Lisa Sood**, VUS, BIS, Vietnam; **Jason Stewart**, Taejon International Language School, South Korea; **Brian A. Stokes**, Korea University, South Korea; **Mulder Su**, Shih-Chien University, Kaohsiung; **Yoomi Suh**, English Plus, South Korea; **Yun-Fang Sun**, Wenzao Ursuline College of Languages, Kaohsiung; **Richard Swingle**, Kansai Gaidai University, Japan; **Sanford Taborn**, Kinjo Gakuin Daigaku, Japan; **Mamoru Takahashi**, Akita Prefectural University, Japan; **Tran Hoang Tan**, School of International Training, Vietnam; **Takako Tanaka**, Doshisha University, Japan; **Jeffrey Taschner**, American University Alumni Language Center, Thailand; **Matthew Taylor**, Kinjo Gakuin Daigaku, Japan; **Michael Taylor**, International Pioneers School, Thailand; **Kampanart Thammaphati**, Wattana Wittaya Academy, Thailand; **Tran Duong The**, Sao Mai Language Center, Vietnam; **Tran Dinh Tho**, Duc Tri Secondary School, Vietnam; **Huynh Thi Anh Thu**, Nhatrang College of Culture Arts and Tourism, Vietnam; **Peter Timmins**, Peter's English School, Japan; **Fumie Togano**, Hosei Daini High School, Japan; **F. Sigmund Topor**, Keio University Language School, Japan; **Tu Trieu**, Rise VN, Vietnam; **Yen-Cheng Tseng**, Chang-Jung Christian University, Tainan; **Pei-Hsuan Tu**, National Cheng Kung University, Tainan City; **Hajime Uematsu**, Hirosaki University, Japan; **Rachel Um**, Mok-dong Oedae English School, South Korea; **David Underhill**, EEExpress, Japan; **Ben Underwood**, Kugenuma High School, Japan; **Siriluck Usaha**, Sripatum University, Thailand; **Tyas Budi Utami**, Indonesia; **Nguyen Thi Van**, Far East International School, Vietnam; **Stephan Van Eycken**, Kosei Gakuen Girls High School, Japan; **Zisa Velasquez**, Taihu International School/Semarang International School, China/Indonesia; **Jeffery Walter**, Sangji University, South Korea; **Bill White**, Kinki University, Japan; **Yohanes De Deo Widyastoko**, Xaverius Senior High School, Indonesia; **Dylan Williams**, SNU, South Korea; **Jisuk Woo**, Ichean University, South Korea; **Greg Chung-Hsien Wu**, Providence University, Taichung; **Xun Xiaoming**, BLCU, China; **Hui-Lien Yeh**, Chai Nan University of Pharmacy and Science, Tainan; **Sittiporn Yodnil**, Huachiew Chalermprakiet University, Thailand; **Shamshul Helmy Zambahari**, Universiti Teknologi Malaysia, Malaysia; **Ming-Yuli**, Chang Jung Christian University, Tainan; **Aimin Fadhlee bin Mahmud Zuhodi**, Kuala Terengganu Science School, Malaysia;

TURKEY **Shirley F. Akis**, American Culture Association/Fomara; **Gül Akkoç**, Boğaziçi University; **Seval Akmeşe**, Haliç University; **Ayşenur Akyol**, Ege University; **Ayşe Umut Aribaş**, Beykent University; **Gökhan Asan**, Kapadokya Vocational College; **Hakan Asan**, Kapadokya Vocational College; **Julia Asan**, Kapadokya Vocational College; **Azarvan Atac**, Piri Reis University; **Nur Babat**, Kapadokya Vocational College; **Feyza Balakbabalar**, Kadir Has University; **Gözde Balikçi**, Beykent University; **Deniz Balım**, Haliç University; **Asli Başdoğan**, Kadir Has University; **Ayla Bayram**, Kapadokya Vocational College; **Pinar Bilgiç**, Kadir Has University; **Kenan Bozkurt**, Kapadokya Vocational College; **Yonca Bozkurt**, Ege University; **Frank Carr**, Piri Reis; **Mengü Noyan Çengel**, Ege University; **Elif Doğan**, Ege University; **Natalia Donmez**, 29 Mayis Üniverste; **Nalan Emirsoy**, Kadir Has University; **Ayşe Engin**, Kadir Has University; **Ayhan Gedikbaş**, Ege University; **Gülşah Gençer**, Beykent University; **Seyit Ömer Gök**, Gediz University; **Tuğba Gök**, Gediz University; **İlkay Gökçe**, Ege University; **Zeynep Birinci Guler**, Maltepe University; **Neslihan Güler**, Kadir Has University; **Sircan Gümüş**, Kadir Has University; **Nesrin Gündoğu**, T.C. Piri Reis University; **Tanju Gurpinar**, Piri Reis University; **Selin Gurturk**, Piri Reis University; **Neslihan Gurutku**, Piri Reis University; **Roger Hewitt**, Maltepe University; **Nilüfer İbrahimoğlu**, Beykent University; **Nevin Kaftelen**, Kadir Has University; **Sultan Kalin**, Kapadokya Vocational College; **Sema Kaplan Rabina**, Anadolu University; **Eray Kara**, Giresun University; **Beylü Karayazgan**, Ege University; **Darren Kelso**, Piri Reis University; **Trudy Kittle**, Kapadokya Vocational College; **Şaziye Konaç**, Kadir Has University; **Güneş Korkmaz**, Kapadokya Vocational College; **Robert Ledbury**, Izmir University of Economics; **Ashley Lucas**, Maltepe University; **Bülent Nedium Uça**, Dogus University; **Murat Nurlu**, Ege University; **Mollie Owens**, Kadir Has University; **Oya Özağaç**, Boğaziçi University; **Funda Özcan**, Ege University; **İlkay Özdemir**, Ege University; **Ülkü Öztürk**, Gediz University; **Cassondra Puls**, Anadolu University; **Yelda Sarikaya**, Cappadocia Vocational College; **Müge Şekercioğlu**, Ege University; **Melis Senol**, Canakkale Onsekiz Mart University, The School of Foreign Languages; **Patricia Sümer**, Kadir Has University; **Rex Surface**, Beykent University; **Mustafa Torun**, Kapadokya Vocational College; **Tansel Üstünloğlu**, Ege University; **Fatih Yücel**, Beykent University; **Şule Yüksel**, Ege University;

THE MIDDLE EAST **Amina Saif Mohammed Al Hashamia**, Nizwa College of Applied Sciences, Oman; **Jennifer Baran**, Kuwait University, Kuwait; **Phillip Chappells**, GEMS Modern Academy, U.A.E.; **Sharon Ruth Devaneson**, Ibri College of Technology, Oman; **Hanaa El-Deeb**, Canadian International College, Egypt; **Yvonne Eaton**, Community College of Qatar, Qatar; **Brian Gay**, Sultan Qaboos University, Oman; **Gail Al Hafidh**, Sharjah Women's College (HCT), U.A.E.; **Jonathan Hastings**, American Language Center, Jordan; **Laurie Susan Hilu**, English Language Centre, University of Bahrain, Bahrain; **Abraham Irannezhad**, Mehre Aval, Iran; **Kevin Kempe**, CNA-Q, Qatar; **Jill Newby James**, University of Nizwa; **Mary Kay Klein**, American University of Sharjah, U.A.E.; **Sian Khoury**, Fujairah Women's College (HCT), U.A.E.; **Hussein Dehghan Manshadi**, Farhang Pajooh & Jaam-e-Jam Language School, Iran; **Jessica March**, American University of Sharjah, U.A.E.; **Neil McBeath**, Sultan Qaboos University, Oman; **Sandy McDonagh**, Abu Dhabi Men's College (HCT), U.A.E.; **Rob Miles**, Sharjah Women's College (HCT), U.A.E.; **Michael Kevin Neumann**, Al Ain Men's College (HCT), U.A.E.;

LATIN AMERICA **Aldana Aguirre**, Argentina; **Claudia Almeida**, Coordenação de Idiomas, Brazil; **Cláudia Arias**, Brazil; **Maria de los Angeles Barba**, FES Acatlan UNAM, Mexico; **Lilia Barrios**, Universidad Autónoma de Tamaulipas, Mexico; **Adán Beristain**, UAEM, Mexico; **Ricardo Böck**, Manoel Ribas, Brazil; **Edson Braga**, CNA, Brazil; **Marli Buttelli**, Mater et Magistra, Brazil; **Alessandra Campos**, Inova Centro de Linguas, Brazil; **Priscila Catta Preta Ribeiro**, Brazil; **Gustavo Cestari**, Access International School, Brazil; **Walter D'Alessandro**, Virginia Language Center, Brazil; **Lilian De Gennaro**, Argentina; **Mônica De Stefani**, Quality Centro de Idiomas, Brazil; **Julio Alejandro Flores**, BUAP, Mexico; **Mirian Freire**, CNA Vila Guilherme, Brazil; **Francisco Garcia**, Colegio Lestonnac de San Angel, Mexico; **Miriam Giovanardi**, Brazil; **Darlene Gonzalez Miy**, ITESM CCV, Mexico; **Maria Laura Grimaldi**, Argentina; **Luz Dary Guzmán**, IMPAHU, Colombia; **Carmen Koppe**, Brazil; **Monica Krutzler**, Brazil; **Marcus Murilo Lacerda**, Seven Idiomas, Brazil; **Cris Lazzerini**, Brazil; **Sandra Luna**, Argentina; **Ricardo Luvisan**, Brazil; **Jorge Murilo Menezes**, ACBEU, Brazil; **Monica Navarro**, Instituto Cultural A. C., Mexico; **Joacyr Oliveira**, Faculdades Metropolitanas Unidas and Summit School for Teachers, Brazil; **Ayrton Cesar Oliveira de Araujo**, E&A English Classes, Brazil; **Ana Laura Oriente**, Seven Idiomas, Brazil; **Adelia Peña Clavel**, CELE UNAM, Mexico; **Beatriz Pereira**, Summit School, Brazil; **Miguel Perez**, Instituto Cultural, Mexico; **Cristiane Perone**, Associação Cultura Inglesa, Brazil; **Pamela Claudia Pogré**, Colegio Integral Caballito / Universidad de Flores, Argentina; **Dalva Prates**, Brazil; **Marianne Rampaso**, Iowa Idiomas, Brazil; **Daniela Rutolo**, Instituto Superior Cultural Británico, Argentina; **Maione Sampaio**, Maione Carrijo Consultoria em Inglês Ltda, Brazil; **Elaine Santesso**, TS Escola de Idiomas, Brazil; **Camila Francisco Santos**, UNS Idiomas, Brazil; **Lucia Silva**, Cooplem Idiomas, Brazil; **Maria Adela Sorzio**, Instituto Superior Santa Cecilia, Argentina; **Elcio Souza**, Unibero, Brazil; **Willie Thomas**, Rainbow Idiomas, Brazil; **Sandra Villegas**, Instituto Humberto de Paolis, Argentina; **John Whelan**, La Universidad Nacional Autonoma de Mexico, Mexico

iv

CONTENTS

UNIT **1**

Business

NOTE TAKING	▶	writing key words and main ideas
LISTENING	▶	listening for key words and phrases
VOCABULARY	▶	distinguishing between words with similar meanings
GRAMMAR	▶	simple present and simple past
PRONUNCIATION	▶	simple past *-ed*
SPEAKING	▶	asking for repetition and clarification

UNIT QUESTION

How can you find a good job?

A Discuss these questions with your classmates.

1. Do you have a job? What is your dream job?

2. How do people find jobs?

3. Look at the photo of a job fair. What types of jobs do you see? Why are the people at this job fair?

B Listen to *The Q Classroom* online. Then answer these questions.

1. Marcus says that the best way to find a job may be through friends. Sophy thinks you should tell everyone you are looking for work. Felix says you have to work your way up. What do you think is the best way to find a job?

2. What experience do you have with these ways of finding a job? Other ways?

 C Go to the Online Discussion Board to discuss the Unit Question with your classmates.

D Match the ads with the jobs in the photos. More than one answer is possible.

1 tempor incidcount ut labore et dolore

Must have excellent computer skills

2 labore et dolore

Need a college education

Email résumé to:

3 Need three years of experience

4 Must enjoy working with people

web designer ____

salesperson ____

server ____

teacher ____

E Tell a partner which job you like best, and why.

A: *I like the web designer job. I have excellent computer skills.*

B: *Really? I prefer the salesperson position. I like working with people.*

When you take notes, you write only a few words and phrases about the most important points. If you try to write too much, you will miss important information. Learn to listen for the main ideas and write the key words and phrases that will help you remember them. Make two columns on your paper and label them *Key Words* and *Main Ideas* as in the example below. As you listen, write the key words in the left column. After you listen, use the key words to fill in additional information about the main ideas in the right column.

Read this transcript from a TV news report about important job skills for university students.

> Many college students today do not have the basic skills needed to succeed in a full-time job after they graduate. According to a recent study, universities need to do more to prepare students for the workplace.

Look at the note page below. Notice the key words and main ideas.

Key Words	Main Ideas
Students don't have skills – full-time job	College students don't have skills to succeed in a full-time job after they graduate.
Study: universities need to prepare students	Study: Universities need to do more to prepare students for work.

A. Listen to the next part of the news report. Make two columns for key words and main ideas. Take notes on the key words.

B. Use the key words you wrote to write the main ideas. Compare notes with a partner.

 C. Go online for more practice with writing notes on key words and main ideas.

LISTENING

LISTENING 1 | Looking for a Job

You are going to listen to two students discuss summer jobs. They find a website with a video called "Careers at Braxton Books." As you listen to the conversation, gather information and ideas about how you can find a good job.

PREVIEW THE LISTENING

A. **VOCABULARY** Here are some words from Listening 1. Read the sentences. Then write each <u>underlined</u> word next to the correct definition.

1. Khalid wants to change his <u>career</u>. He wants to become a doctor.

2. Haya starts her new job tomorrow. She's a new <u>employee</u> of that company.

3. A college education is one <u>requirement</u> to be a teacher. You also need some teaching experience.

4. I don't know much about computers. I can only do <u>basic</u> things, like type papers and use email.

5. Our server isn't very <u>organized</u>. He forgot to bring your coffee, and he brought me the wrong food.

6. Education is important. It's harder to get some jobs if you don't have a college <u>degree</u>.

7. I want to get a job at Rick's Café. I just have to complete this <u>application</u> and take it to the restaurant.

8. I have an <u>interview</u> next week at a computer company.

a. _____ (*noun*) a person who works for someone

b. _____ (*noun*) a paper you get when you finish college

c. _____ (*noun*) a job that you learn to do and then do for many years

d. _____ (*noun*) a special piece of paper you fill out when you try to get a job

e. _____ (*noun*) something that you need or that you must do or have

f. _____ (*adjective*) able to plan your work or life well

g. _____ (*noun*) a meeting when someone asks you questions to decide if you will get a job

h. _____ (*adjective*) simple; including only what is necessary

B. Go online for more practice with the vocabulary.

C. PREVIEW **Two students are looking online for a summer job. They find a website with a video called "Careers at Braxton Books."**

Check (✓) the topics you think the video will include.

☐ how to buy books online   ☐ how to get an application

☐ job requirements   ☐ store hours

WORK WITH THE LISTENING

A. LISTEN AND TAKE NOTES **Listen to the conversation. Take notes on the key words. Follow the sample notes on page 5.**

B. Listen to the conversation again. Add notes about the main ideas based on the key words you wrote.

C. Read the statements. Write *T* (true) or *F* (false). Then correct any false statements. Write the words or phrases from your notes that helped you get the answer.

_F_ **1.** Ben works at Braxton Books now.

Ben doesn't work at Braxton Books yet.

Words and phrases: _wants to work there this summer_

____ **2.** Braxton Books is a big company.

_____

Words and phrases: _____

____ **3.** The company sells books in stores and online.

_____

Words and phrases: _____

____ **4.** The company has some open jobs.

_____

Words and phrases: _____

___ 5. Ben will probably try to get a job at Braxton Books.

_____

Words and phrases: _____

D. Circle the answer that best completes each statement.

1. Braxton Books plans to ___ .
   a. open a new store   b. continue its success   c. start an e-book business

2. Salespeople at Braxton Books have to ___ .
   a. work only online   b. have a college degree   c. help a lot of customers

3. Most Web designers at Braxton Books are ___ .
   a. highly trained   b. college students   c. friendly people

4. The company only accepts applications ___ .
   a. on its website   b. in person   c. after an interview

E. Match the sentence halves to form true statements.

___ 1. Ben is looking for   a. a salesperson position.

___ 2. Braxton Books is   b. a summer job.

___ 3. You need basic computer skills for   c. to work on a team.

___ 4. Web designers need   d. an international company.

___ 5. A new part of Braxton's business is   e. a lot of experience.

___ 6. Salespeople must like   f. an e-book business.

Tip for Success

Speakers sometimes use certain phrases to signal a list of important information. Some examples are *here are,* *the following are,* and *here is a list of.*

F. Listen to the excerpt from Listening 1. Complete the job requirements for each job in the chart.

Salesperson	Web designer
• _____ years' experience	• _____ years' experience
• basic _____	• _____ skills
• organized	• _____ in Web design
• friendly	(preferred)
• enjoy _____	• organized
_____	• have _____ ideas

SAY WHAT YOU THINK

Discuss the questions in a group.

Critical Thinking **Tip**

Question 1 asks you to **compare** the two jobs. **Comparing** means you notice the things that are the same for both jobs. Comparing can help you remember important points about the two things.

1. Look again at the chart in Activity F on page 8. What requirements are necessary for both jobs at Braxton Books?

2. Do you meet the requirements for the jobs? Which ones?

3. Which student in your group is the best person for each job at Braxton Books?

Listening Skill | **Listening for key words and phrases**

Key words and **phrases** tell you the important information about a topic. Speakers often repeat key words and phrases more than once. Listening for key words and phrases can help you identify the topic of a conversation.

Listen to the example from Listening 1.

The topic of the conversation is *looking for a summer job*.

The key words and phrases are *work there this summer*, *job*, and *careers*. The speakers say the words *summer* and *jobs* more than once.

A. Ben and Saud are listening to the information video for Braxton Books. Listen for key words and phrases in each section. Circle the main topic.

1. a. careers at Braxton Books
   b. the company's history and success
   c. the number of employees

2. a. jobs at Braxton Books
   b. how to get an application
   c. job interviews

3. a. store hours
   b. computer skills
   c. job requirements

4. a. job interviews
   b. how to get an application
   c. how to buy online books

B. Listen again. Check (✓) the words and phrases the speaker uses more than once.

1. ☐ interest in careers
   ☐ growing
   ☐ over 200 stores
   ☐ success

2. ☐ job
   ☐ positions
   ☐ great people
   ☐ join our team

3. ☐ requirements
   ☐ college degree
   ☐ years of experience
   ☐ interesting

4. ☐ interested
   ☐ one of our stores
   ☐ application
   ☐ interview

C. Go online for more practice with listening for key words and phrases.

LISTENING 2 | The Right Person for the Job

UNIT OBJECTIVE ▶▶▶ You are going to listen to the manager of an advertising company. He is interviewing two people for a Web designer position. As you listen to the interviews, gather information and ideas about how you can find a good job.

PREVIEW THE LISTENING

A. VOCABULARY Here are some words from Listening 2. Read their definitions. Then complete each sentence below with the correct word.

> **advertising** (*noun*) telling people about things to buy
>
> **assistant** (*noun*) a person who helps someone in a more important position
>
> **graduate** (*verb*) to finish your studies at a school, college, or university
>
> **major** (*noun*) the main subject you study in college
>
> **manager** (*noun*) 🔑 the person who controls a company or business
>
> **résumé** (*noun*) a list of your education and work experience that you send when you are trying to get a job

🔑 Oxford 2000 keyword

1. My mother speaks French very well. French was her _____ in college.

2. Juan got a job as a(n) _____ in a school. He'll help the children when the teacher is busy.

3. It isn't easy to get a job in _____. You need to have interesting ideas, and you have to know how to sell things.

4. I sent my _____ to ten companies. Only one company called me for an interview.

5. My father is the _____ of a large restaurant. He has a lot of employees, and he's very busy.

6. I plan to _____ from college next year.

iQ ONLINE **B.** Go online for more practice with the vocabulary.

C. PREVIEW You are going to listen to Mark Williamson, the manager of New World Design Advertising Company. He is going to interview Tom and George for a Web designer position.

Check (✓) the interview questions you think Mark will ask.

☐ Can you tell me a little about yourself?
☐ What was your major in college?
☐ How old are you?
☐ Do you have any experience in advertising?
☐ What are your best qualities?
☐ Are you married?
☐ Do you have any questions?

Tip for Success

Remember to listen for key words and phrases. They will help you know the topics of the interview.

WORK WITH THE LISTENING

A. LISTEN AND TAKE NOTES In the first interview, Mark interviews Tom. Listen and take notes on the key words. See the sample below.

Mark	Tom
Tell me about yourself.	Came to NY from Chicago

B. In the second interview, Mark interviews George. Listen and take notes on the key words.

C. Listen to both interviews again. What does each person say about his education, experience, and skills? Write notes in the chart.

	Education	Experience	Skills
1. Tom			
2. George			

D. Read the sentences. Circle the word or phrase that best completes each sentence.

1. The company is in (New York / Chicago / London).

2. Tom has a lot of (design experience / computer skills / questions).

3. In college, Tom worked at a (company / restaurant / store).

4. Mark does not ask Tom about his (résumé / personality / experience).

5. George says he was very (busy / organized / friendly) in college.

6. George has a good (job / personality / idea) for the position.

E. Complete each sentence with a word from the box. You will use some words more than once.

education   experience   skills

1. Tom talks mostly about his _____ .

2. Tom has a lot of useful _____ for Web design.

3. Tom does not have the _____ necessary for the job.

4. George has _____ as an office assistant in an advertising agency.

5. George's _____ does not relate to advertising.

F. Read the sentences. Then check (✓) *True, Probably true, Probably not true,* or *Not true.*

	True	Probably true	Probably not true	Not true
1. Tom graduated from college.	☐	☐	☐	☐
2. Tom wishes he had more experience.	☐	☐	☐	☐
3. Mark will choose Tom for the job.	☐	☐	☐	☐
4. George's college major was design.	☐	☐	☐	☐
5. George enjoys working with people.	☐	☐	☐	☐
6. George is the right person for the job.	☐	☐	☐	☐

 G. Go online to listen to *What Makes a Good Manager?* and check your comprehension.

 # SAY WHAT YOU THINK

A. Discuss the questions in a group.

1. Which person should get the job in Listening 2? Why?

   A: I think ... should get the job. ... He has ...
   B: I disagree. I think ...

2. Have you ever been on a job interview? What other questions can people ask?

B. Before you watch the video, discuss the questions in a group.

1. What special skills do you need for the job you want?

2. How can people learn new job skills?

 C. Go online to watch the video about learning new skills to get a job. Then check your comprehension.

> **make a living** *(phr. v.)* earn money to buy the things you need in life
> **pathway** *(n.)* a way to achieve something
> **training** *(v.)* making yourself ready for something by studying or doing something a lot

VIDEO VOCABULARY

D. Think about the unit video, Listening 1, and Listening 2 as you discuss the questions.

1. What steps do people take to find a job?

2. With your group, think of three interesting jobs. What are the best ways to find out about job openings and the best ways to train for each job?

Distinguishing between words with similar meanings

Some words have **similar meanings**, but they are used in different situations. The definitions and example sentences in the dictionary can help you decide which word is best to use.

Look at the dictionary entries and example sentences for *career* and *work*.

---

ca·reer 🔑 /kəˈrɪr/ *noun* [*count*]
a job that you learn to do and then do for many years: *He is considering a **career in** teaching.* ◆ *His career was always more important to him than his family.* ⊃ Look at the note at **job**.

work² 🔑 /wərk/ *noun*
1 [*noncount*] the job that you do to earn money: *I'm looking for work* ◆ *What time do you **start work**?* ◆ *How long have you been **out of work** (= without a job)?* ⊃ Look at the note at **job**.

> Max graduated from college last year. He's ready to start a **career**.
> I have to leave for **work** very early tomorrow morning.

The definition of *career*, as you can see, is a job you want or plan to do for a long time. *Work* is a more general word meaning the job you do for money.

Always look for both words in the dictionary before deciding which one to use.

All dictionary entries are from the *Oxford Basic American Dictionary for learners of English* © Oxford University Press 2011.

A. Read the dictionary entries. Circle the best word for each sentence.

---

job 🔑 **AWL** /dʒɑb/ *noun* [*count*]
1 the work that you do for money: *She got a job as a waitress.* ◆ *Peter just lost his job.*

ca·reer 🔑 /kəˈrɪr/ *noun* [*count*]
a job that you learn to do and then do for many years: *He is considering a **career in** teaching.* ◆ *His career was always more important to him than his family.* ⊃ Look at the note at **job**.

---

1. A (job / career) in law can be very demanding.

2. My company closed. I need to find another (job / career) soon.

| **com·pa·ny** 🔑 /ˈkʌmpəni/ *noun* (plural com·pa·nies)
1 [*count*] (**BUSINESS**) a group of people who work together to make or sell things: *an advertising company* • *the Student Loans Company* ➲ The short way of writing "Company" in names is Co.: *Milton and Co.*
2 [*noncount*] being with a person or people: *I always enjoy Mark's company.* | **busi·ness** 🔑 /ˈbɪznəs/ *noun* (plural busi·ness·es)
1 [*noncount*] buying and selling things: *I want to go into business when I leave school.* • *Business is not very good this year.*
2 [*noncount*] the work that you do as your job: *The manager will be away on business next week.* • *a business trip* |

3. Jim went into (company / business) with his brother.

4. The (company / business) has over 6,000 employees around the world.

B. Write one new sentence for each word in Activity A.

1. (job) _____

_____

2. (career) _____

_____

3. (company) _____

_____

4. (business) _____

_____

C. Go online for more practice with distinguishing between words with similar meanings.

SPEAKING

 **UNIT OBJECTIVE** ▶▶▶▶ At the end of this unit, you are going to role-play a job interview with a partner using the interview questions on page 23. As you speak, you will need to ask for repetition and clarification.

Grammar | *Part 1* Simple present

- Use the simple present to talk about facts or general truths.

    Braxton Books **is** a big company.   I **enjoy** working with people.

Simple present statements with regular verbs

Affirmative	Negative
I / You **like** working on a team.	I / You **do not like** this job.
He / She / It **wants** to change careers.	He / She / It **does not want** to be a manager.
We / You / They **sell** computers.	We / You / They **do not sell** advertising.

- Use the simple present to describe habits and routines.

    We **take** the train to the office.   I **do not work** on Fridays.

Simple present statements with *be*

Affirmative	Negative
I **am** friendly.	I **am not** a server.
You **are** organized.	You **are not** organized.
He / She / It **is** on time.	He / She / It **is not** on time.
We / You / They **are** college students.	We / You / They **are not** employees.

- Use the simple present to describe states and feelings.

    You **are** very friendly.   I **want** a career as a Web designer.

Simple present statements with *have*

Affirmative	Negative
I / You **have** a college degree.	I / You **do not have** a résumé.
He / She / It **has** a few questions.	He / She / It **does not have** the application.
We / You / They **have** 600 employees.	We / You / They **do not have** an office in New York.

A. Circle the correct verb to complete each sentence.

1. A Web designer (need / needs) a lot of experience, but I only (have / has) one year.

2. It (is not / does not) easy to find a job these days, especially if you (want / wants) a good career.

3. I (have / has) a college degree, and I (am / is) a hard worker.

4. The company does not (accept / accepts) applications online. They (prefer / prefers) to meet you in person.

5. The manager (like / likes) your résumé, but we (do not / does not) have any open positions.

6. She (are not / is not) very organized, but she (enjoy / enjoys) working on a team.

Use the **simple past** to talk about actions that happened in the past.

Regular verbs
- To form the simple past, add **-ed** to the base form of the verb.

  I work**ed** at a clothing store last summer. I help**ed** customers.

- For verbs ending in *e*, add **-d**.

  I serve**d** dinner at a busy restaurant. I also prepare**d** takeout orders.

- For verbs ending in *y*, drop the *y* and add **-ied**.

  Tom app**lied** for a position as a Web designer. He stud**ied** Web design in college.

Irregular verbs

The verb *be* is irregular in the simple past. It has two forms: ***was*** and ***were***.

  My internship **was** a good experience. The people I worked with **were** great.

Here are some other verbs with irregular simple past forms.

say	**said**	have	**had**	come	**came**
make	**made**	know	**knew**	see	**saw**
go	**went**	take	**took**	get	**got**
do	**did**				

> **Negative statements**
> - To form a negative statement, use *didn't* + the base form of the verb.
>
> ☐ I **didn't graduate** from high school last year. It was two years ago.

A. Complete each sentence with the simple past form of the verb.

Mark: Well, let's get started. Please sit down, Tom. . . . OK. Can you tell me a little about yourself?

Tom: Sure. I _____ to New York a few months ago from
1. (come)

Chicago. I _____ to Chicago School of Design.
2. (go)

Mark: Yes, I _____ that on your résumé. Yes, here it is. You
3. (see)

_____ last May. What did you study there?
4. (graduate)

Tom: I'm sorry. I didn't catch that. Could you say that again, please?

Mark: Sure. What _____ your major in college?
5. (be)

Tom: Well, I _____ my degree in design. I _____
6. (get)   7. (take)

a lot of computer classes, too. I _____ to use my design
8. (want)

and computer skills. That's why I want a career in Web design.

B. Practice the conversation in Activity A with a partner.

C. Read the notes an interviewer wrote about Carlos. Then read the interview questions below. Write your own answers to the questions.

1. from Caracas, Venezuela; graduated from Central University in 2009

2. major was computer science, studied English

3. was a Web designer for one year; before that, was a waiter

1. Can you tell me a little about yourself?

2. What did you study in high school/college?

3. What work experience do you have?

D. Take turns asking and answering the job interview questions in Activity C with your partner. Use your notes.

E. Go online for more practice with the simple present and the simple past.

F. Go online for the grammar expansion.

| Pronunciation | Simple past -*ed* |

The simple past of a regular verb ends in -*ed*. The pronunciation of this final sound depends on the sound at the end of the base verb. There are three possible sounds.

- The -*ed* = /d/ when the sound is **voiced** (with sound). This includes all vowel sounds, and the consonants /b/, /g/, /dʒ/ (ju**dg**ed), /l/, /m/, /n/, /r/, /v/, and /z/.

- The -*ed* = /t/ when the sound is **unvoiced** (without sound), including /f/, /k/, /p/, /s/, /ʃ/ (wi**sh**), and /tʃ/ (wat**ch**).

- The -*ed* = /əd/ when the final sound is either the voiced sound /d/ or the unvoiced sound /t/.

 Read and listen to the examples in the chart.

If the verb ends in . . .	Base verb	Simple past
• a voiced sound, pronounce the past with /d/.	enjoy	enjoy**ed**
	study	stud**ied**
	learn	learn**ed**
• an unvoiced sound, pronounce the past with /t/.	laugh	laugh**ed**
	work	work**ed**
	help	help**ed**
	wash	wash**ed**
• a /t/ or /d/, pronounce the past with /əd/.	graduate	graduat**ed**
	end	end**ed**

A. Work with a partner. Take turns saying the simple past forms of the verbs in the box.

change	like	need	require	study	walk
complete	look	prefer	stop	wait	want

B. Write the simple past form of each verb in Activity A in the correct column. Then listen and check your answers.

/t/	/d/	/əd/
	changed	

C. Read the conversations and <u>underline</u> the regular verbs in the simple past. Write /d/, /t/, or /əd/ above each verb ending to tell its correct pronunciation.

1. A: I <u>completed</u> /əd/ an application for a job at Jim's Pizza today.

   B: Oh, I worked at Jim's Pizza last summer. I washed dishes there.
   It was fun.

   A: Really? That's good. I wanted to work at Paul's Café, but they said
   I needed more experience.

   B: Yeah, they chose someone else for the job.

   A: Who?

   B: Me.

2. A: Please sit down, Mr. Smith. Did you bring your application?

   B: I completed it online, and I emailed it. Is that OK?

   A: Oh, yes. Here it is. I printed it this morning. . . . Now, can you tell
   me a little about yourself?

   B: Yes, I graduated from Franklin High School in 2010. I wanted to
   get some work experience before college. So, I joined a computer
   training program.

   A: I see. Did you finish the program?

   B: Yes, I finished it last week.

D. Practice the conversations in Activity C with your partner. Check your partner's pronunciation of the simple past.

 **E.** Go online for more practice with pronouncing the simple past with -*ed*.

When you listen, sometimes you need to ask the speaker to repeat information. Here are some phrases you can use when you don't hear or understand something well.

I'm sorry. I didn't catch that.	Could you say that again, please?
Could you repeat that?	Do you mean . . . ?

A. Listen to the excerpt from Listening 2. Check (✓) the phrases Tom uses.

☐ I didn't catch that.   ☐ Could you say that again, please?
☐ Could you repeat that?   ☐ Do you mean . . . ?

B. Listen and complete each conversation with a phrase for repetition and clarification.

1. **Miteb:** Hello?

   Fahad: Hello, is this Miteb?

   Miteb: Yes, it is.

   Fahad: Oh, hi, Miteb. It's Fahad from All-Tech Computers. Thank you for coming to the interview this morning. I forgot to ask you about . . .

   Miteb: Hello? _____.

2. **Interviewer:** Great. OK, thanks. And can you tell me a little about your experience in Australia? I saw on your résumé that . . .

   Liam: _____?

3. **Waleed:** Hey, Jamal! How are you doing?

   Jamal: Oh, hi, Waleed. I'm great! I just found out that . . .

   Waleed: Sorry, Jamal. _____?

4. **Andrew:** What do you plan to do after you graduate, Seth?

   Seth: Well, I had a meeting with the manager of New World Designs last week.

   Andrew: A meeting? _____?

Tip for Success

It may be impolite in some cultures, but it's important to ask for clarification in English-speaking countries when you don't understand something. Begin with *I'm sorry* or *excuse me* to be more polite.

C. Take turns reading the conversations in Activity B with a partner.

D. Go online for more practice with asking for repetition and clarification.

In this assignment, you are going to role-play a job interview with a partner. As you prepare your role-play, think about the Unit Question, "How can you find a good job?" Use information from Listening 1, Listening 2, the unit video, and your work in the unit to support your role-play. Refer to the Self-Assessment checklist on page 24.

CONSIDER THE IDEAS

A. Work with a partner. Match each job with the correct advertisement.

___ 1. office assistant   ___ 4. children's sports coach

___ 2. tour guide   ___ 5. house painter

___ 3. video game tester   ___ 6. high school English teacher

A Must have college degree in teaching and two years of experience working in a school.
www.QHS_K-12.edu

HELP WANTED

B Must be friendly and organized. Excellent speaking skills. **Must speak English, French, and Spanish.**

Email résumé to: **jo@citytours.com**

C Requirements: excellent computer skills, online game experience.
www.game-on.org

D Experience playing soccer, baseball, and basketball. Must be very friendly.

Complete an application at **www.sports4kidz.org**

E Must be organized. Need excellent computer skills. One to two years of experience.
Come in to the office and complete an application. **215 Green Street**

F NO EXPERIENCE NEEDED. **Must enjoy working outdoors on big projects. For applications, call (802) 555-2191**

B. Read the ads again. <u>Underline</u> the job requirements for each ad.

C. Work in a group. Which jobs in Activity A do you want to have? Do you meet the requirements? Tell your group.

"I want to be an office assistant. I'm organized and have good computer skills."

PREPARE AND SPEAK

A. **GATHER IDEAS** Work with a partner. Think of a job you want to have. Together, list the requirements for that job and your partner's job.

B. **ORGANIZE IDEAS** Imagine you are going to an interview for your job from Activity A. The interviewer asks you these questions. How do you answer?

1. Can you tell me a little about yourself? _____

   _____

2. What did you study in high school or college? _____

   _____

3. What work experience do you have? _____

   _____

4. What skills do you have? _____

   _____

5. Do you have any questions? _____

   _____

C. **SPEAK** Role-play the interview with your partner. Use the interview questions from Activity B. Take notes on your partner's answers. Refer to the Self-Assessment checklist on page 24 before you begin.

A: Hello, I'm _____. Please have a seat.

B: Thank you. It's nice to meet you, _____.

A: OK. Let's get started.

   (Question 1) _____

B: (Answer) _____

A: (Question 2) _____

B: (Answer) _____

A: (Question 3) _____

B: (Answer) _____

A: (Question 4) _____

B: (Answer) _____

A: (Question 5) _____

B: (Answer) _____

 Go online for your alternate Unit Assignment.

CHECK AND REFLECT

A. CHECK Think about the Unit Assignment as you complete the Self-Assessment checklist.

SELF-ASSESSMENT		
Yes	**No**	
☐	☐	I was able to speak easily about the topic.
☐	☐	I took notes on key words and main ideas.
☐	☐	My partner/group/class understood me.
☐	☐	I used statements in the simple present and the simple past.
☐	☐	I used vocabulary from the unit.
☐	☐	I asked for repetition and clarification.
☐	☐	I pronounced the simple past of regular verbs correctly.

 B. REFLECT Go to the Online Discussion Board to discuss these questions.

1. What is something new you learned in this unit?

2. Think about the Unit Question—How can you find a good job? Is your answer different now than when you started the unit? If yes, how is it different? Why?

TRACK YOUR SUCCESS

Circle the words and phrases you have learned in this unit.

Nouns
advertising
application
assistant AWL
business 🔑
career 🔑
company 🔑
degree 🔑
employee
interview 🔑
job 🔑
major AWL
manager 🔑
requirement AWL
résumé
work 🔑

Verb
graduate

Adjectives
basic 🔑
organized 🔑

Phrases
Could you repeat that?
Could you say that
  again, please?
Do you mean . . . ?
I'm sorry. I didn't
  catch that.

🔑 Oxford 2000 keywords
AWL Academic Word List

Check (✓) the skills you learned. If you need more work on a skill, refer to the page(s) in parentheses.

NOTE TAKING ■	I can take notes on key words and main ideas. (p. 5)
LISTENING ■	I can listen for key words and phrases. (p. 9)
VOCABULARY ■	I can use the dictionary to distinguish between words with similar meanings. (p. 14)
GRAMMAR ■	I can recognize and use the simple present and the simple past. (pp. 16 and 17)
PRONUNCIATION ■	I can pronounce simple past -ed endings. (p. 19)
SPEAKING ■	I can ask for repetition and clarification. (p. 21)
UNIT OBJECTIVE ▶▶▶▶ ■	I can gather information and ideas to role-play a job interview.

UNIT 2	NOTE TAKING ▶ taking notes in a T-chart
Cultural Studies	LISTENING ▶ listening for main ideas and details
	VOCABULARY ▶ words in context
	GRAMMAR ▶ *should/shouldn't; it's* + adjective + infinitive
	PRONUNCIATION ▶ the schwa /ə/ sound
	SPEAKING ▶ presenting information from notes

UNIT QUESTION

Why do we study other cultures?

A Discuss these questions with your classmates.

1. Did you ever spend time in another country or culture?

2. What are some ideas people around the world have about your country or culture?

3. Look at the photo. Where do you think this is? What do you think the people are doing?

Listen to a lecture and three stories. Gather information and ideas to give a presentation about customs in a culture you know well.

◉ **B** Listen to *The Q Classroom* online. Then match the ideas in the box with the students.

a. We learn from them.

b. It's interesting.

c. ~~People are different.~~

d. It helps us live peacefully.

Why do we study other cultures?	
Marcus	*c. People are different.*
Yuna	
Felix	
Sophy	

 C Go to the Online Discussion Board to discuss the Unit Question with your classmates.

D What are some things that make your culture different from other cultures? Write your ideas in the chart.

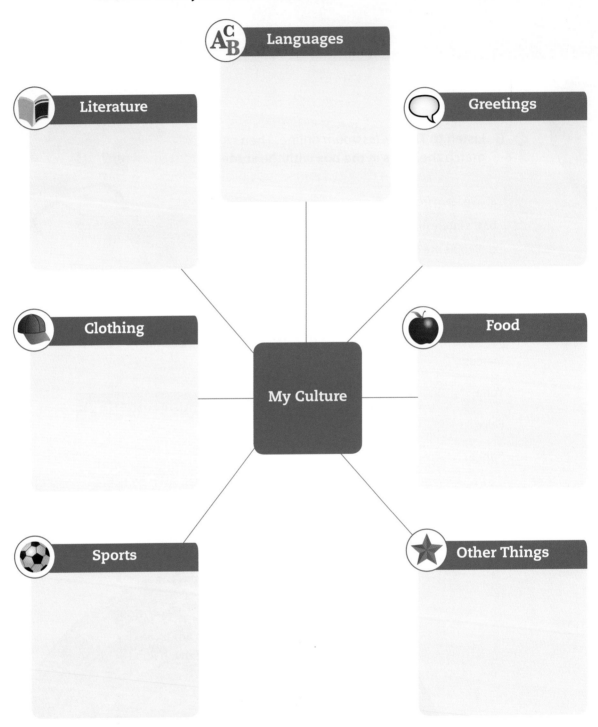

Languages

Literature

Greetings

Clothing

Food

My Culture

Sports

Other Things

E Work in a group. Use your chart from Activity D and present one interesting fact about your culture to your group.

"In my country, people bow when they greet each other."

You can use a **T-chart** to organize your notes. In Unit 1, you organized key words and main ideas in two columns, similar to a T-chart. Now you will use a T-chart to take notes on main ideas and details. Details include examples, numbers, facts, names, and reasons. Write the main ideas on the left and the details on the right.

Read the information about culture shock from an international student handbook. Then look at a student's T-chart below.

> Spending time in a different culture can be difficult. International students may experience "culture shock." This is especially common during the first few months after they arrive in a new place. The term *culture shock* describes an uncomfortable feeling that comes from being in a new environment far from home. Signs of culture shock differ from person to person and may include feeling sad, homesick, sleepy, or angry.

Main Ideas	Details
• International students: may have culture shock	• Common during first few months
• Culture shock: uncomfortable feeling when far from home	• Signs: feeling sad, homesick, sleepy, angry

 **A.** Listen to the beginning of a presentation about culture shock for new international university students. Take notes in the chart as you listen.

Tip for Success

To identify the main ideas, remember to listen for key words and phrases.

Main Ideas	Details

B. Compare notes with a partner.

 C. Go online for more practice with taking notes in a T-chart.

LISTENING 1 | International Advertising

UNIT OBJECTIVE ▶▶▶▶

You are going to listen to a lecture from a business class at a university. The professor is talking about international advertising. As you listen to the lecture, gather information and ideas about why we study other cultures.

PREVIEW THE LISTENING

A. **VOCABULARY** Here are some words from Listening 1. Read the conversations below. Then match each <u>underlined</u> word with its definition.

Tip for Success

Form a "study group" with some classmates to discuss things you learn in class.

a. when a life finishes

b. a problem

c. to try not to do something

d. something that you do that is wrong

e. something a group of people usually do

f. between different countries

g. the lowest part of something

h. thinking or talking about the good parts of a situation

Vocabulary Skill Review

In Unit 1, you learned how to distinguish between words with similar meanings. Look at the vocabulary words in Activity A. Do you know any other words with similar meanings?

____ 1. **A:** I started a job at a great company.
   B: Oh, where is it?
   A: Well, it's an <u>international</u> company. They have offices around the world.

____ 2. **A:** I lived in Europe for six months.
   B: Really? What was it like?
   A: Well, I had <u>difficulty</u> understanding the culture, but I really enjoyed it.

____ 3. **A:** I made a big <u>mistake</u> at work.
   B: Oh, no. What did you do?
   A: I called my new boss by his first name. He looked very angry.

____ 4. **A:** Do colors have different meanings in different cultures?
   B: Yes. Sometimes a color has a good or <u>positive</u> meaning in one culture and a bad meaning in another culture.

____ 5. **A:** There are different ideas around the world about <u>death</u>.
   B: What do you mean?
   A: I mean, in some countries people wear black and are very sad, but in others people celebrate.

Oxford 2000 keywords

___ 6. **A:** In Korea, do people take off their shoes when they enter their homes?
       B: Yes, it's a Korean <u>custom</u>.

___ 7. **A:** I'm going to India on business. Do you have any travel advice?
       B: Yes. <u>Avoid</u> using your left hand. For example, it's very impolite to shake hands or eat with your left hand.

___ 8. **A:** In the Middle East, you shouldn't show the <u>bottom</u> of your shoes.
       B: Why not?
       A: Shoes are dirty. It's not polite.

iQ ONLINE **B.** Go online for more practice with the vocabulary.

C. **PREVIEW** You are going to listen to a university business class. The professor is giving a lecture about international advertising and the problems companies have when advertising in different countries. Check (✓) the problems you think advertisers have.

☐ language mistakes
☐ problems with colors
☐ problems with numbers
☐ problems with different customs

WORK WITH THE LISTENING

A. **LISTEN AND TAKE NOTES** Listen to the lecture. Make a T-chart and, in the left column, take notes on the main ideas. Use the sample notes below to help you.

Lecture: International Advertising

Main Ideas	Details
• Language mistakes can cause problems for companies.	• Product name has funny or strange meaning in another language

B. Listen again. Add any important details in the right column of your T-chart. Then compare notes with a partner.

C. Complete the statements about the lecture with information from the box. Use your notes to help you.

colors	lose money
international advertising	make cultural mistakes
learn about the customs	product name

1. International companies sometimes _____ in advertising.

2. Language differences can be a problem in _____.

3. A _____ may have a funny meaning in another language.

4. Some _____ are not good to use in advertisements.

5. Companies sometimes _____ because of advertising mistakes.

6. To avoid problems, companies should _____ of other countries.

D. The professor gives two examples of international advertising mistakes. Write notes to complete the chart about the mistakes.

	Type of company	Where the mistake happened	Mistake
Example 1			
Example 2			

E. Read the statements. Write *T* (true) or *F* (false). Correct any false statements.

___ 1. The computer company did not change the product name.

_____

___ 2. The color red usually has a positive meaning.

_____

___ 3. Companies should avoid the color blue in advertising.

_____

___ 4. The colors black and green can both mean death.

_____

F. Circle the answer that best completes each statement. Use information from the listening and your own ideas.

1. Today there are more ___ than in the past.
    a. advertising companies
    b. colors in advertising
    c. international companies

2. It is important for companies to learn about other countries' cultures ___.
    a. because they may be the same
    b. before they advertise there
    c. when they buy their products

3. When international companies understand other cultures, they ___.
    a. probably lose less money
    b. may have problems in the future
    c. don't advertise internationally

SAY WHAT YOU THINK

Discuss the questions in a group.

1. What do companies need to think about when they advertise in other countries? Give an example from your experience. Think about the problems with language, color, and customs in Listening 1.

2. What colors have special meaning in your country?

When you listen, focus on the main ideas (the most important points about the topic) and any important details. Remember that details include examples, numbers, facts, names, and reasons. Ask yourself, "What information is important for me to know?"

Lecture: International Advertising

Main Ideas	Details
• Language mistakes can cause problems for companies.	• Product name has funny or strange meaning in another language

A. Listen to an excerpt from a lecture. Complete the T-chart with the missing information.

Lecture: International Advertising

Main Idea	Details
International companies should _____ _____	• Numbers _____ in one culture, bad in another
	• Some languages in _____, word for 4 _____ _____
	• Ex: company put 4 _____ _____ in package, no one in _____ bought them

B. Listen to another excerpt from a lecture. Take notes in the T-chart. Then compare notes with a partner.

Main Ideas	Details

 C. Go online for more practice with listening for main ideas and details.

LISTENING 2 | Cultural Problems

 **UNIT OBJECTIVE**

You are going to listen to three people talking about cultural problems. As you listen to the stories, gather information and ideas about why we study other cultures.

PREVIEW THE LISTENING

A. **VOCABULARY** Here are some words from Listening 2. Read their definitions. Then complete each sentence below with the correct word. Change the verb form if you need to.

> **carefully** (*adverb*) 🔑 a way of doing something so you don't make a mistake
>
> **confused** (*adjective*) 🔑 not able to think clearly; not understanding
>
> **die** (*verb*) 🔑 to stop living
>
> **invite** (*verb*) 🔑 to ask someone to come somewhere or to do something
>
> **offended** (*adjective*) angry or unhappy because someone does something you don't think is polite
>
> **rude** (*adjective*) 🔑 not polite
>
> **upset** (*adjective*) 🔑 unhappy or worried
>
> **wedding** (*noun*) 🔑 a special event when two people get married

🔑 Oxford 2000 keywords

1. There's a new student from Turkey in our English class.

   Let's _____ him to our house for dinner tomorrow.

2. I saw Lisa crying after class. She looked very _____.

3. Susan was an hour late, and she didn't call. Isn't that very

   _____?

4. In the Middle East, you should always say yes when someone offers you

   something. If you say no, the person may be _____.

5. In some countries, it's common to wear black when someone

   _____.

6. Colors are an important part of a _____. Many women

   wear a white dress, but in some countries, women wear red.

7. I didn't understand English well when I visited Ireland. When people spoke, I felt a little _____. But I still had a great time.

8. Watch people _____. Then you won't make a mistake.

B. Go online for more practice with the vocabulary.

C. PREVIEW You are going to listen to three people telling about cultural problems. Look at the photos. What cultural problem do you think each shows?

WORK WITH THE LISTENING

A. LISTEN AND TAKE NOTES Listen to Joao, Tanya, and Rick tell their stories. Use a T-chart to take notes on the main ideas and details of each story.

B. Compare notes with a partner.

C. Read the sentences. Then listen again. Circle the word or phrase that best completes each sentence.

1. Joao's story happened in (his home country / a store / a university class).

2. In Brazil, it is probably (rude / confusing / OK) to stand close to other people.

3. Tanya felt (positive / confused / upset) about her trip to Canada.

4. Russians often give flowers when someone (takes a trip / dies / is offended).

5. People in the United States usually use business cards when they (meet someone new / do business / take a trip).

6. Some guests at Rick's friend's wedding were probably (offended / rude / working).

D. Match the information in the box with the person.

attended a special event	is a university student in the U.S.
did not make a cultural mistake	offended someone in a shop
enjoyed meeting a friend's family	went to another country for business

Joao	
Tanya	
Rick	*attended a special event*

E. Read the questions. Then circle the correct answer.

1. Which statement is true about Joao's story?
    a. He offended a very close friend.
    b. He did not know he was rude until later.
    c. The custom is also rude in his culture.

2. Which statement describes Tanya's experience?
    a. She was upset when her coworkers gave her six flowers.
    b. She did not understand why her coworkers gave her gifts.
    c. She was not offended by the cultural mistake.

3. Which statement is true about Rick's experience?
    a. He did something that was not polite.
    b. He thought the other guests were very rude.
    c. He brought his business cards to the wedding.

4. What is true about all three people?
    a. They are all university students.
    b. They all made a cultural mistake.
    c. They all learned something important.

F. Complete the sentences with your own ideas and compare answers with a partner. Then check your answers with another pair.

1. The student at the bookstore was upset because Joao _____

   _____.

2. Joao didn't know what was wrong. He felt _____

   _____.

3. Tanya's coworkers gave her gifts because _____

   _____.

4. Tanya thinks some other Russians might _____

   _____.

5. In Russia, it's OK to _____.

6. Rick learned that in Japan, you should always _____

   _____.

 G. Go online to listen to *My Grandmother* and check your comprehension.

 SAY WHAT YOU THINK

A. Discuss the questions in a group.

1. Do you know any of the customs from Listening 2? Read each statement and check (✓) *Yes* or *No*. Then discuss your answers.

	Yes	No
1. In my culture, it's rude to stand very close to someone.	☐	☐
2. Some numbers in my culture have a special meaning.	☐	☐
3. In my culture, people only use business cards in business situations.	☐	☐

2. Do you have an example of a cultural problem? Tell your classmates the story.

B. Before you watch the video, discuss the questions in a group.

1. Think about your country and culture a long time ago. What are some things that are different now from the past?

2. What are some things that are still the same?

C. Go online to watch the video about Shanghai, China. Then check your comprehension.

D. Think about the unit video, Listening 1, and Listening 2 as you discuss the questions.

1. What problems can happen when people don't know about another culture?

2. What are some important things people from other cultures should know about your culture?

Vocabulary Skill   Words in context

When you listen, you will sometimes hear words you don't know. You can use other information to help you guess the meaning of new words. This is called **context**. The words that come before and after another word are the context.

> Then he looked very upset and said, "Excuse me!" and moved away.
> I didn't know what was wrong. I was **confused**. I learned later that . . .

You can guess the meaning of *confused* from the context. The speaker says, "I didn't know what was wrong." *Confused* is a feeling. (The speaker says, "I <u>was</u> *confused*.") You can guess that *confused* is a feeling that you have when you don't understand.

A. Listen to a student's story about living in Australia. Use the context to guess the meaning. Circle the correct meaning of each word.

1. **depressed**
   a. very sad
   b. very offended

2. **tough**
   a. enjoyable; fun
   b. difficult or challenging

3. **considerate**
   a. caring; thoughtful
   b. rude and unkind

4. **treated**
   a. avoided
   b. behaved toward

5. **optimistic**
   a. cheerful; positive
   b. stressful and worried

Ayers Rock, Australia

B. Listen again. Write any words or phrases that helped you get the meaning. Compare answers with a partner.

1. first time away, miss my family _____

2. _____

3. _____

4. _____

5. _____

 C. Go online for more practice with words in context.

SPEAKING

UNIT
OBJECTIVE
At the end of this unit, you are going to give a presentation about customs in a culture you know well. As you give your presentation, you will need to present information from your notes.

Grammar   Part 1 *Should* and *shouldn't*

To form a sentence, use a **subject** + *should/shouldn't* + **the base form of a verb.**

I	
You	
He / She	**should** learn customs of other countries.
We	**shouldn't** make too many cultural mistakes.
You	
They	

Note: *Shouldn't* is the contraction of *should* + *not*.

Use *should* to say that it is good to do something.

☐ In Japan, you **should** take a business card with two hands.

When something is <u>not</u> good to do, we use *shouldn't*.

☐ You **shouldn't** give six or eight flowers in Russia.

A. What do you know about customs from around the world? Circle *should* or *shouldn't*. Then listen and check your answers.

1. In India, you (should / shouldn't) use your left hand to eat.

2. In Vietnam, you (should / shouldn't) touch a person on the head.

3. In the U.S., you (should / shouldn't) look at people's eyes when you speak to them.

4. In France, when you visit someone's home, you (should / shouldn't) bring a gift.

5. In Saudi Arabia, you (should / shouldn't) say no when someone offers you something to eat or drink.

6. In Colombia, you (should / shouldn't) avoid giving marigolds—a yellow flower—as a gift.

B. What are things you should or shouldn't do in your culture? Write two sentences with *should* and two sentences with *shouldn't*. Then read your sentences to a partner.

1. _____

2. _____

3. _____

4. _____

Grammar | *Part 2* It's + adjective + infinitive

You can make statements with *it's* + (*not*) **adjective** + **infinitive** to talk about behavior and customs. The infinitive is *to* + the base form of a verb.

> **It's polite to say** "thank you."
> **It's rude to show** the bottom of your feet.
> **It's common to wear** a white wedding dress.
> **It's not common to wear** a green wedding dress.
> **It's OK to use** your first name.
> **It's not OK to use** your short name.

Note: *It's* is the contraction of *it + is*.

A. Listen to the excerpts from Listening 2. Fill in the blanks with the missing information.

1. There was another student standing in front of the shelf. I stood next to him and started to look for my book. Then he looked very upset and said, "Excuse me!" and moved away. I didn't know what was wrong. I was confused. I learned later that you shouldn't stand very close to other people in the U.S. _____.

2. They gave me some very nice gifts . . . and they gave me flowers—six flowers. In Russia, _____ of flowers, for example, one, three, five. . . . But you shouldn't give two, four, or six flowers. We only do that when a person dies.

3. I was a little surprised. In the U.S., we only use cards for business, so I didn't bring mine. I just took the Japanese people's business cards and put them in my pocket. After the wedding, I learned that _____. You should always take the cards with two hands and read them carefully. I only used one hand, and I didn't read them at all!

B. **What are customs in your culture or another culture you know? Write one sentence for each topic in the box. Use *it's* + (*not*) adjective + infinitive.**

eating/drinking	greetings	visiting someone's home
gestures	holidays	workplace/office

1. _____

2. _____

3. _____

4. _____

5. _____

6. _____

C. **Work in a group. Take turns reading your sentences. Ask questions if you don't understand.**

D. **Go online for more practice with *should* and *shouldn't* and *it's* + adjective + infinitive.**

E. Go online for the grammar expansion.

Pronunciation **The schwa /ə/ sound**

The **schwa /ə/** is the most common vowel sound in English. It sounds like the *a* in *about* /əˈbaʊt/. We pronounce the vowel in many unstressed syllables (or parts of words) with the schwa /ə/ sound. The schwa /ə/ is never in a stressed syllable.

In these examples, the vowels in red are pronounced with a schwa /ə/ sound.

    avoid   cultural   custom   international   problem

A. Listen and repeat these words. Then <u>underline</u> the schwa sound in each word.

1. avoid
2. bottom
3. considerate
4. offended
5. personality
6. positive
7. similar
8. telephone

B. Write four sentences. In each sentence, use a word from Activity A. Then take turns reading your sentences with a partner.

1. _____

2. _____

3. _____

4. _____

 C. Go online for more practice with the schwa /ə/ sound.

Speaking Skill	Presenting information from notes

When you present information to an audience, you should not read directly from your notes. It's important to look up and make eye contact with the audience. This makes the presentation more interesting.

Preparation

- Use small cards.
- Write only key words and phrases. Don't write the whole presentation.
- Practice your presentation.

Presentation

- Look at the audience. Then begin speaking.
- Look down briefly to check your notes.
- Make eye contact with individual people in your audience as you speak.

Tip for Success

Before you give a presentation, practice it several times. Try standing in front of a mirror. Practice speaking from notes and making eye contact until you feel comfortable.

A. Read the Web page with tips for visiting Egypt. <u>Underline</u> the key words and phrases for each tip.

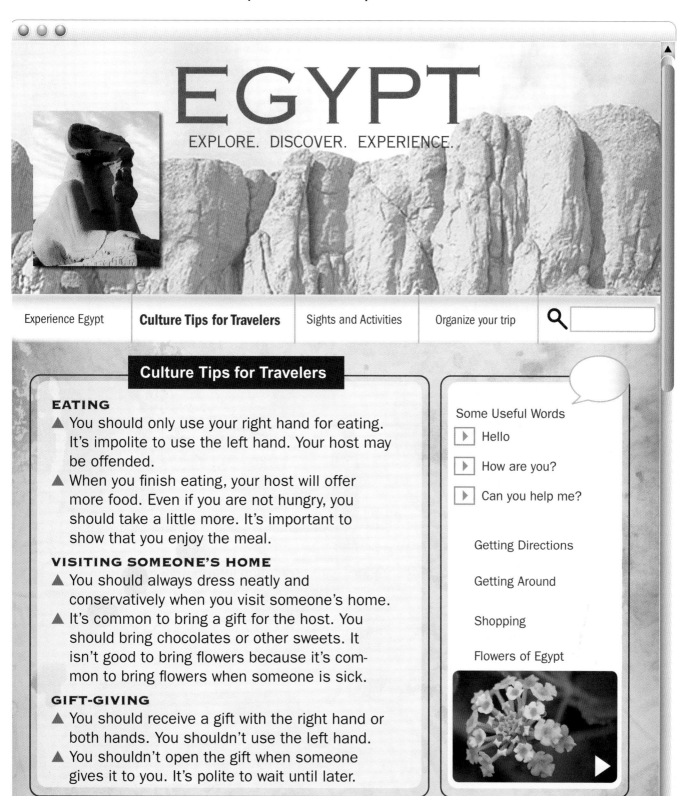

EGYPT
EXPLORE. DISCOVER. EXPERIENCE.

| Experience Egypt | **Culture Tips for Travelers** | Sights and Activities | Organize your trip |

Culture Tips for Travelers

EATING
- ▲ You should only use your right hand for eating. It's impolite to use the left hand. Your host may be offended.
- ▲ When you finish eating, your host will offer more food. Even if you are not hungry, you should take a little more. It's important to show that you enjoy the meal.

VISITING SOMEONE'S HOME
- ▲ You should always dress neatly and conservatively when you visit someone's home.
- ▲ It's common to bring a gift for the host. You should bring chocolates or other sweets. It isn't good to bring flowers because it's common to bring flowers when someone is sick.

GIFT-GIVING
- ▲ You should receive a gift with the right hand or both hands. You shouldn't use the left hand.
- ▲ You shouldn't open the gift when someone gives it to you. It's polite to wait until later.

Some Useful Words
- ▶ Hello
- ▶ How are you?
- ▶ Can you help me?

Getting Directions

Getting Around

Shopping

Flowers of Egypt

Culture Tips for Visiting Egypt Presentation Notes

1. _____ Eating _____

   - only use _____ your right hand _____

   - impolite to use _____

   - host will _____;

     you should _____

2. _____ someone's home

   - _____ and conservatively

   - bring _____,

     such as _____

   - do NOT bring _____

3. _____

   - receive a gift _____

   - do NOT use _____

   - should wait to _____

C. Work with a partner. Take turns presenting the information in Activity B. Be sure to look at your partner when you speak.

 D. Go online for more practice with presenting information from notes.

UNIT OBJECTIVE ▶▶▶▶ In this assignment, you are going to plan and give a presentation about your culture or another culture you know well. As you prepare your presentation, think about the Unit Question, "Why do we study other cultures?" Use information from Listening 1, Listening 2, the unit video, and your work in the unit to support your presentation. Refer to the Self-Assessment checklist on page 48.

CONSIDER THE IDEAS

Look again at the web page on page 45. Discuss these questions in a group.

1. Are any of the customs in Egypt similar to customs you know? Which ones?

2. Do you think it's important to learn the customs of a country you visit? Why or why not?

PREPARE AND SPEAK

A. GATHER IDEAS Choose three topics from the box and write them in the T-chart below. Complete the T-chart with notes about customs in your culture or another culture you know well.

business	gestures	greetings
eating and drinking	gift-giving	visiting someone's home

Topic	Customs
1.	
2.	
3.	

Critical Thinking **Tip**

In Activity B, you are going to **prepare** your presentation. **Preparing** a presentation on a topic involves applying your knowledge in a new way or doing something new.

B. **ORGANIZE IDEAS** Use your notes from the T-chart in Activity A to prepare a short presentation about customs in your culture or another culture you know well. Write your presentation notes on note cards.

C. **SPEAK** Give your presentation to the class (or to a group). Use your note cards during the presentation, and remember to look at your audience. Refer to the Self-Assessment checklist below before you begin.

 Go online for your alternate Unit Assignment.

CHECK AND REFLECT

A. **CHECK** Think about the Unit Assignment as you complete the Self-Assessment checklist.

SELF-ASSESSMENT		
Yes	**No**	
☐	☐	I was able to speak easily about the topic.
☐	☐	I used a T-chart to take notes on main ideas and details.
☐	☐	My partner/group/class understood me.
☐	☐	I used *should/shouldn't* and *it's* + (*not*) adjective + infinitive correctly.
☐	☐	I used vocabulary from the unit.
☐	☐	I presented information from notes.
☐	☐	I correctly pronounced any words with schwa /ə/.

 B. **REFLECT** Go to the Online Discussion Board to discuss these questions.

1. What is something new you learned in this unit?

2. Look back at the Unit Question—Why do we study other cultures? Is your answer different now than when you started the unit? If yes, how is it different? Why?

TRACK YOUR SUCCESS

Circle the words you have learned in this unit.

Nouns
bottom 🔑
custom 🔑
death 🔑
difficulty 🔑
mistake 🔑
wedding 🔑

Verbs
avoid 🔑
die 🔑
invite 🔑
treat 🔑

Adjectives
confused 🔑
considerate
depressed AWL

international 🔑
offended
optimistic
positive 🔑 AWL
rude 🔑
tough
upset 🔑

Adverb
carefully 🔑

🔑 Oxford 2000 keywords
AWL Academic Word List

Check (✓) the skills you learned. If you need more work on a skill, refer to the page(s) in parentheses.

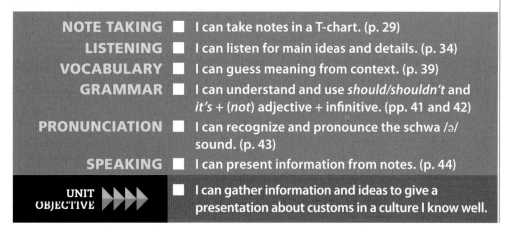

NOTE TAKING ☐	I can take notes in a T-chart. (p. 29)
LISTENING ☐	I can listen for main ideas and details. (p. 34)
VOCABULARY ☐	I can guess meaning from context. (p. 39)
GRAMMAR ☐	I can understand and use *should/shouldn't* and *it's* + (*not*) adjective + infinitive. (pp. 41 and 42)
PRONUNCIATION ☐	I can recognize and pronounce the schwa /ə/ sound. (p. 43)
SPEAKING ☐	I can present information from notes. (p. 44)
UNIT OBJECTIVE ▶▶▶▶ ☐	I can gather information and ideas to give a presentation about customs in a culture I know well.

NOTE TAKING ▶	marking important information in notes
LISTENING ▶	understanding numbers and dates
VOCABULARY ▶	suffixes *-ful* and *-ing*
GRAMMAR ▶	*be going to*
PRONUNCIATION ▶	reduction of *be going to*
SPEAKING ▶	introducing topics in a presentation

UNIT QUESTION

What is the best kind of vacation?

A Discuss these questions with your classmates.

1. What did you do on your last vacation?

2. What are popular places for tourists in your home country?

3. Look at the photo. Where are these people? Is this the kind of vacation you would go on?

UNIT ▶▶▶▶
OBJECTIVE

Listen to a lecture and a presentation. Gather information and ideas to participate in a presentation describing a travel tour.

B Listen to *The Q Classroom* online. Then answer these questions.

1. Yuna says she prefers a relaxing beach vacation. What kinds of vacations do Sophy and Felix prefer?

2. Which student's opinion do you agree with? Why?

iQ ONLINE **C** Go online to watch the video about popular tourist places. Then check your comprehension.

VIDEO VOCABULARY

lifetime *(n.)* a person's entire life

market *(n.)* a place where people buy food, clothing, or other goods

tourist attraction *(n.)* a place where many people come to visit

iQ ONLINE **D** Go to the Online Discussion Board to discuss the Unit Question with your classmates.

E Work with a partner. Look at each sign. What does it mean? What are some locations where you might see it?

Meaning: _____

_____

Locations: _____

_____

Meaning: _____

_____

Locations: _____

_____

Meaning: _____

_____

Locations: _____

_____

Meaning: _____

_____

Locations: _____

_____

Meaning: _____

_____

Locations: _____

_____

Meaning: _____

_____

Locations: _____

_____

F Look again at the signs in Activity E. Discuss these questions in a group.

1. Why do you think the signs were put up?

2. Do you think people need signs like these? Why or why not?

3. Can you think of examples of similar signs? Draw or explain one to your group.

When you take notes, it is helpful to mark specific details or information. For example, you can <u>underline</u>, box, circle, or star (✻) important facts, names, numbers, or dates. This will make it easy to find and remember the information in your notes later.

You can also use **symbols** to mark your feelings as you take notes. For example, use an exclamation point (!) for a surprising fact or a question mark (?) for something you don't understand. You can check your questions later and add to your notes.

Listen to the beginning of a lecture about Costa Rica. Read the student's notes and notice the marking.

> Lecture: Costa Rica
> Located in Central America
> Borders <u>Nicaragua</u>, <u>Panama</u>, <u>Pacific Ocean</u>,
> <u>Caribbean Sea</u>
> 16th-18th centuries – Spanish rule✻
> Independent country – Sept. 21, 1821
> Popular for tourists = 2 million/year!

A. Listen to the next part of the presentation about Costa Rica. Take notes as you listen.

B. Look at your notes and mark the important information with symbols. Then compare notes with a partner.

C. Go online for more practice with marking important information in notes.

LISTENING 1 | Places in Danger

You are going to listen to a report from a travel program. As you listen to the report, gather information and ideas about what the best kind of vacation is.

PREVIEW THE LISTENING

A. **VOCABULARY** Here are some words from Listening 1. Read their definitions. Then complete each sentence below with the correct word. Change nouns to plural if you need to.

Tip for Success

Pay attention to the listening title. Think about it before you start listening. Ask yourself, *What is this about? What do I know about this topic?*

dangerous (*adjective*) 🔑 may hurt you

destroy (*verb*) 🔑 to break or ruin something

insect (*noun*) 🔑 a small animal with six legs, such as an ant or a fly

local (*adjective*) 🔑 of a place near you

pollution (*noun*) 🔑 dirty air or water

shake (*verb*) 🔑 to move quickly up and down or from side to side

tourist (*noun*) 🔑 a person who visits a place on vacation

🔑 Oxford 2000 keywords

1. If you travel to Mexico, you should try the _____ food. Tacos are my favorite dish.

2. Suddenly, the building started to _____. We all ran outside.

3. Too many visitors could _____ these very old houses.

4. Many big cities have problems with _____. Cars and buses make the air dirty.

5. Many countries need _____ to help the local economy.

6. Do you think it's _____ to travel alone?

7. What kind of _____ is that? It's such a colorful bug.

 B. Go online for more practice with the vocabulary.

C. PREVIEW You are going to listen to a report from a travel program called *Places in Danger*. The program talks about the negative effects of tourists visiting three famous places. Look at these places. What do you know about them? Why do you think they are in danger?

1
the Great Wall of China

2
the Galapagos Islands, Ecuador

3
Antarctica

WORK WITH THE LISTENING

A. LISTEN AND TAKE NOTES Listen to the presentation. Take notes on the effects of tourism in each of the three places: the Great Wall of China, the Galapagos Islands, and Antarctica. Use the example below to guide you.

Great Wall	Galapagos Islands	Antarctica
runs across	in Pacific Ocean,	first tourists – 1956
north of China	near S. America	

B. Look at your notes. Mark the important information. Follow the examples of marking and symbols on page 53. Then compare notes with a partner.

C. Listen again. What problems do tourists cause at each place? Fill in the blanks with the missing information.

	Problems caused by tourists
Great Wall of China	Millions of _____ _____. Buses and cars _____.
Galapagos Islands	Planes and boats sometimes _____.
Antarctica	Tourist business causes _____, changes _____, and causes problems for _____.

D. Look at these signs. Where would tourists see them: at the Great Wall of China, the Galapagos Islands, or Antarctica? Write the name of the place under each sign.

_____   _____   _____

E. Listen again. Complete the sentences that explain what people are doing to protect each place.

1. Great Wall of China: Many areas _____ .

2. Galapagos Islands: Airlines must _____

    _____ .

3. Antarctica: Tourists cannot _____ .

    They cannot move or take _____ .

    They must wash _____ .

F. Read the statements. Write *T* (true) or *F* (false). Then correct any false statements.

____ 1. The Great Wall is open to visitors every day.

        _____

____ 2. Tourists drive cars and buses on top of the Great Wall.

        _____

____ 3. Of all three places, the Great Wall gets the most visitors each year.

        _____

____ 4. The Galapagos Islands are home to thousands of people.

        _____

_____ 5. The number of tourists to Antarctica is growing.

SAY WHAT YOU THINK

Discuss the questions in a group.

1. Were you surprised about the problems at these places? Why or why not?

2. Think of one more idea to help each place. Then share it with the class.

3. Name some famous places in your country. Do tourists cause any problems there?

Listening Skill | **Understanding numbers and dates**

It's important to understand numbers when you listen; for example, when you listen to detailed information on a TV or radio program or during a lecture.

Numbers ending in *-teen* or *-ty* can be difficult. You need to listen carefully for the stress patterns in these numbers. That way you can be sure you understand the numbers correctly.

- **In numbers ending in -ty,** the first syllable is stressed: FIF-ty.
- **In numbers ending in -teen,** the stress is on the last syllable: fif-TEEN.

Listen to these pairs of numbers.

14 / 40   15 / 50   16 / 60   17 / 70   18 / 80   19 / 90

Listen to these large numbers.

453	four hundred fifty-three
3,227	three thousand two hundred twenty-seven
15,609	fifteen thousand six hundred nine
275,000	two hundred seventy-five thousand
8,250,000	eight million two hundred fifty thousand

Listen to these dates.

1700 → seventeen hundred   1989 → nineteen eighty-nine
1809 → eighteen oh nine   2011 → twenty eleven (two thousand eleven)

Tip for Success

To practice listening for numbers and dates, watch the news in English every day. If you watch videos of the news online, you can repeat them many times.

A. Listen to excerpts from Listening 1. Complete the student's notes below with the missing information.

Great Wall of China	Runs _____ kilometers across north
	Some parts over _____ years old
	About _____ tourists/day
	(_____ visitors/year)
Galapagos Islands	_____ main islands – home to thousands of plants and animals
	About _____ tourists/year
Antarctica	First tourists arrived in _____
	Only about _____ visitors/year
	then Today, close to _____

B. Mark the important information and details in the notes. Then compare notes with a partner.

C. Complete the travel quiz with a partner. Then listen and check your answers.

What do you know about the world?
Take this travel quiz, and find out!

1. Mount Everest is ____ meters high.
   a. 850
   b. 8,850
   c. 9,580

2. The Eiffel Tower in Paris was built in ____.
   a. 1599
   b. 1702
   c. 1889

3. Burj Khalifa, the tallest building in the world, is ____ meters tall.
   a. 828
   b. 880
   c. 8,018

4. The population of New York City is about ____.
   a. 83,000
   b. 8,300,000
   c. 63,000,000

5. There are ____ islands in the Philippines.
   a. 717
   b. 7,107
   c. 71,000

6. Angel Falls in Venezuela is the world's tallest waterfall. It's ____ meters tall.
   a. 979
   b. 1,065
   c. 2,500

A: I think Mount Everest is 8,850 meters high. What do you think?

B: I'm not sure. Maybe it's nine thousand . . .

D. Go online for more practice with understanding numbers and dates.

LISTENING 2 | A Helpful Vacation

You are going to listen to the owner of a travel company give a presentation about jobs for volunteers in Cusco, Peru. As you listen to the presentation, gather information and ideas about what the best kind of vacation is.

PREVIEW THE LISTENING

Vocabulary Skill Review

In Unit 2, you learned about finding the meaning of new words through the context. Try to find the meaning of the vocabulary words in Activity A by looking at the context.

A. **VOCABULARY** Here are some words from Listening 2. Read the sentences. Circle the answer that best matches the meaning of each underlined word.

1. After college, Yolanda wants to work as a <u>volunteer</u>.
   a. someone who works without pay   b. someone who does difficult work

2. We really enjoyed our trip to Europe. We saw lots of <u>pretty</u> towns and took some great pictures.
   a. dangerous   b. beautiful

3. China has the largest <u>population</u> of all the world's countries. In some cities, you could have millions of "neighbors"!
   a. number of people   b. number of buildings

4. The Mada'in Saleh is an <u>ancient</u> site. No one knows exactly who built it.
   a. very small   b. very old

5. I'm going to Morocco tomorrow, so I have to pack my bags and <u>prepare</u> for my trip.
   a. get ready   b. get tired

6. We waited in the airport for a long time. There was a problem with the airplane and they had to <u>repair</u> it.
   a. fix   b. destroy

7. In the summer, I work as a tour guide. I <u>lead</u> tourists to interesting places in my hometown.
   a. take   b. shake

8. I love to travel and learn about different cultures. It's very <u>enjoyable</u>.
   a. not fun   b. fun

iQ ONLINE   **B.** Go online for more practice with the vocabulary.

C. **PREVIEW** Volunteer Vacations is a travel company that offers work and travel around the world. You are going to listen to the owner of the company giving a presentation about jobs for volunteers in Cusco, Peru.

Look at the pictures. Check (✓) the activities you think the volunteers will do.

1 ☐

visit Machu Picchu

2 ☐

paint a school

3 ☐

volunteer as a teacher

4 ☐

go to a Peruvian beach

WORK WITH THE LISTENING

A. **LISTEN AND TAKE NOTES** Listen to the presentation and complete the student's notes.

> *Cusco – population _____, near Andes Mountains*
>
> *_____ hours by train to Machu Picchu ✳ (visit end of first week!)*
>
> *Trip is from June _____ to July _____*
>
> *Live with _____*
>
> *Volunteer work: help _____, may _____ English!*

B. Compare notes with a partner. Listen again and correct any errors in your notes.

C. Each of these statements is false. Correct them.

1. Cusco, Peru is a small town near the Andes Mountains.

   _____

2. The volunteers will visit Machu Picchu after four weeks.

   _____

3. The volunteers will travel to Peru during April and May.

   _____

4. The group will live at a local school.

   _____

5. For work, the volunteers will repair houses.

   _____

6. They may teach Spanish to children at a school.

   _____

D. Match the sentence halves to form true statements.

___ 1. Machu Picchu is a good place to

___ 2. During the first two weeks the group will

___ 3. The main goal of the volunteers is to

___ 4. The volunteers may

a. study the language and culture of Peru.

b. learn about ancient history.

c. teach their own language.

d. help the local people.

E. Read the sentences. Then check (✓) *True* or *False*. If the information is not in the presentation, check *It doesn't say.*

	True	False	It doesn't say.
1. All of the volunteers are university students.	☐	☐	☐
2. The volunteer work will begin the first week.	☐	☐	☐
3. Some of the host families can speak English.	☐	☐	☐
4. The volunteers will work in a new school.	☐	☐	☐
5. This is the travel company's first trip to a school.	☐	☐	☐

F. Compare answers with a partner. Correct any false statements.

 G. Go online to listen to *The Peace Boat* and check your comprehension.

SAY WHAT YOU THINK

A. Discuss the questions in a group.

1. Do you think this volunteer tour sounds like an exciting vacation? Why or why not?

2. Do you want to take a volunteer tour? Where do you want to go?

3. How can you help in another place?

B. Think about the unit video, Listening 1, and Listening 2 as you discuss the questions.

1. What are some of the good and bad effects of tourists visiting famous places? Add more good and bad effects to the T-chart below.

Good	Bad
brings money to local people	causes pollution

2. What activities can volunteers do to help the people in your country or where you live?

Suffixes are letters or groups of letters at the end of a word. Suffixes can change the tense (*-ed*, *-ing*), the number (*-s*, *-es*), or the part of speech of a word. Learning different suffixes is a good way to build your vocabulary.

- The suffix *-ful* changes a noun to an adjective.

  beauty → beautiful   The Burj Al Arab is a **beautiful** building.
  wonder → wonderful   The restaurants in Dubai are **wonderful**.

- The suffix *-ing* can change a verb to an adjective.

  excite → exciting   Tokyo is an **exciting** place. There are many fun things to do.
  interest → interesting   Our visit to Machu Picchu was very **interesting**.

A. Read the sentences. Write the adjective form of each word in parentheses.

1. If you go to Peru, you should visit Machu Picchu. The old stone

   buildings are _____ (amaze).

2. Until about 1920, the Galapagos Islands were very _____

   (peace). Only animals lived there, no people.

3. Sometimes tourists can be _____ (help) to the place they

   visit. They create jobs for local people.

4. We visited Venice, Italy during our last vacation. It is a very

   _____ (charm) city.

5. I don't want to just go to the beach for my vacation. I want to do

   something _____ (meaning), like volunteer work.

6. The Great Wall of China is in danger because of the _____

   (rise) number of tourists.

7. Did you enjoy your volunteer tour? I want to take one next year. I heard

   it's a very _____ (interest) experience.

8. Many areas of the Great Wall of China are now closed to visitors.

   It's very fragile, so you have to be _____ (care).

B. Write four sentences about a tourist place you visited. Use the words to form adjectives with *-ing* or *-ful*.

1. _____
   (wonder)

2. _____
   (amaze)

3. _____
   (excite)

4. _____
   (beauty)

C. Share your sentences with a partner. Ask follow-up questions about the vacations or places.

A: Beijing is a wonderful city.
B: Oh, when did you go there?
A: Last summer. It was hot there.

A view of downtown Beijing, China

 D. Go online for more practice with the suffixes *-ful* and *-ing*.

UNIT OBJECTIVE At the end of this unit, you are going to work in a group to plan and present a travel tour. As you give your presentation, you will need to introduce topics.

Grammar   *Be going to*

Be going to statements

We use *be going to* + **the base form of a verb** to talk about the future, usually about our future plans.

> Tomorrow we**'re going to visit** the Great Wall of China.
> I**'m going to take** a volunteer tour this summer.

- To form the future with *be going to*, use *am*, *is*, or *are* + *going to* + the base form of the verb.

> She **is going to study** Spanish for two weeks.
> They **are going to repair** a school in Peru.

- To make a negative statement, use *not* before *going to*.

> I **am not going to stay** in a hotel.
> We **are not going to go** shopping today.

- In speaking and informal writing, we often use contractions.

> John**'s going to fly** to the Galapagos Islands in the morning.
> The museum **isn't going to be** open tomorrow.

Be going to questions

- Form *yes/no* questions by changing the order of the subject and *be*.

> They **are going to** volunteer in Peru.
> **Are they going to** volunteer in Peru?

- Form information questions by adding the *wh-* word and changing the order of the subject and *be*.

> **Where are they going to** volunteer?

A. Read the email about a tree-planting tour in Nepal. Complete the sentences with the correct form of *be going to* and the verbs in parentheses. Use contractions.

To:	ken_fujiwaka@getmail.com
From:	jon.miller22@greatmail.com
Subject:	Summer plans

Hi Ken,

I'm writing to tell you about my exciting summer plans. ___I'm going to join___ a
                                                                  1. (join)

volunteer tour to Nepal! Here are some of the things we _____.
                                                             2. (do)

On the first day we _____ a bus to Gorkha, the old capital of
                                           3. (take)

Nepal. It _____ a long trip—five hours! I hope it doesn't rain.
                         4. (be)

The tour website says that on a clear day, you can see Mount Everest from

the bus window! We _____ three days hiking and camping in
                              5. (spend)

the Himalayas. Our guide _____ us about the mountain plants
                              6. (teach)

and animals. Then our group _____ in a small town and help
                              7. (stop)

the local people plant trees. I think that _____ the most
                              8. (be)

enjoyable part of the trip. Well, I have to go.

I _____ a blog, so you can
          9. (write)
read all about the trip!

Take care,

Jon

B. Match the questions with the answers. Then listen to the conversations and check your answers.

_____ 1. What are you going to do in China?

a. No, we're going to go shopping.

_____ 2. Where are we going to stay?

b. Yes, he's going to go to Hawaii.

_____ 3. Can we go to the National Museum today?

c. We're going to return on May 16th.

_____ 4. How long is your trip?

d. You're going to live with a local family.

_____ 5. Is John going to take a vacation this year?

e. I'm going to do volunteer work in Shanghai.

C. Write questions. Use _be going to_. Then ask and answer the questions with a partner.

1. What/you/do this weekend

   What are you going to do this weekend ?

2. you/study English/this weekend

   _____ ?

3. What/you/do/during the next holiday

   _____ ?

4. Where/you/travel/next summer?

   _____ ?

iQ ONLINE   **D. Go online for more practice with _be going to_.**

E. Go online for the grammar expansion.

When using *be going to*, speakers, especially in the United States, often pronounce *going to* as *gonna*. They reduce the sounds.

Listen and repeat these sentences. The speaker reads them twice. Pay attention to the pronunciation of *going to* the first time you hear each sentence, and the pronunciation of *gonna* the second time.

1. We're going to visit Italy next year.
2. She isn't going to come with us.
3. I'm going to stay with a family in Madrid.
4. They aren't going to join a tour.

Note: We never write *gonna* in academic or professional writing.

A. Write answers to the questions. Use *be going to*. Then take turns asking and answering the questions with a partner. Use the reduced pronunciation of *going to*.

1. A: When are you going to take your next vacation?

   B: _____.

2. A: Where are you going to go?

   B: _____.

3. A: Who are you going to travel with?

   B: _____.

4. A: What are you going to do there?

   B: _____.

B. Imagine you are going to take a volunteer tour. Use the questions in Activity A to plan your trip. Ask and answer the questions about your trip with your partner.

 C. Go online for more practice with the reduction of *be going to*.

When you give a presentation, you want it to be organized so that your audience can follow what you are saying. Here are some useful phrases for organizing a presentation.

- To introduce the first topic:

  Let's start with . . .
  The first thing I'm going to talk about is . . .

- To change to a new topic:

  Now let's move on to . . .
  Next, I'm going to talk about . . .

- To introduce the last topic:

  Finally, let's talk about . . .
  To wrap up, I'm going to tell you about . . .

- To introduce the next speaker (when there is more than one):

  Now Pamela is going to tell you about . . .
  Now Jun Ho is going to take over.

Critical Thinking

Activity A asks you to **decide** on the best order. You decide by looking at everything you know about a subject. **Deciding** helps you put information together in a useful way.

A. Work with a partner. Imagine you work for a tour company. You are going to present a tour to a group of tourists. Decide on the best order to present these topics. Number them 1 to 6.

____ the cost of the trip

____ the first day

____ the flight information

____ the food

____ the schedule of places to visit

____ the volunteer activities

B. Take turns with your partner making sentences from the phrases in the Speaking Skill box above and the topics in Activity A. Follow the order you decided on in Activity A.

"The first thing I'm going to talk about is the schedule. . . ."

 C. Go online for more practice with introducing topics in a presentation.

UNIT OBJECTIVE ▶▶▶▶ In this assignment, you are going to work in a group to plan a vacation for tourists and then present the tour to your class. As you prepare your presentation, think about the Unit Question, "What is the best kind of vacation?" Use information from Listening 1, Listening 2, the unit video, and your work in the unit to support your presentation. Refer to the Self-Assessment checklist on page 72.

CONSIDER THE IDEAS

A. Listen to two tour guides present information about a tour to Nepal. Number the topics in order.

___ activities

___ cost

___ food

___ lodging

___ schedule

B. Listen again and take notes on the details for each topic in Activity A. Then compare notes with a partner.

PREPARE AND SPEAK

A. GATHER IDEAS Work in a group. Imagine you work for a tour company.

1. Choose a travel destination and plan a tour to that place. Think of a place you know well or do some research on a new destination.

2. Take notes including information on schedule, lodging, food, activities, and cost.

 **Tip** for Success

Here are some useful phrases for adding information when a co-presenter is speaking: *May I say one more thing? / I'd like to add one point. / Can I add something?*

B. ORGANIZE IDEAS With your group, plan a presentation to give information about your tour. Plan to use visuals such as a poster or photos in your presentation. Decide who will talk about each topic. Use your notes from Activity A.

C. SPEAK Practice your presentation. Then give your presentation to the class (or to a group). Refer to the Self-Assessment checklist below before you begin.

Go online for your alternate Unit Assignment.

CHECK AND REFLECT

A. CHECK Think about the Unit Assignment as you complete the Self-Assessment checklist.

SELF-ASSESSMENT		
Yes	No	
☐	☐	I was able to speak easily about the topic.
☐	☐	I marked important information in my notes.
☐	☐	My partner/group/class understood me.
☐	☐	I used *be going to* correctly.
☐	☐	I used vocabulary from the unit.
☐	☐	I introduced topics in a presentation.
☐	☐	I pronounced *be going to* correctly.

 B. REFLECT Go to the Online Discussion Board to discuss these questions.

1. What is something new you learned in this unit?

2. Think about the Unit Question—What is the best kind of vacation? Is your answer different now than when you started the unit? If yes, how is it different? Why?

TRACK YOUR SUCCESS

Circle the words and phrases you have learned in this unit.

Nouns
insect 🔑
pollution 🔑
population
tourist 🔑
volunteer AWL

Verbs
destroy 🔑
lead 🔑
prepare 🔑
repair 🔑
shake 🔑

Adjectives
ancient 🔑
dangerous 🔑
enjoyable 🔑
local 🔑
pretty 🔑

Phrases
Let's start with . . .
The first thing I'm going
   to talk about is . . .
Now let's move on to . . .
Next, I'm going
   to talk about . . .
Now (name) is going to
   tell you about . . .
Now (name) is going to
   take over.
Finally, let's talk
   about . . .
To wrap up, I'm going to
   tell you about . . .

🔑 Oxford 2000 keywords
AWL Academic Word List

Check (✓) the skills you learned. If you need more work on a skill, refer to the page(s) in parentheses.

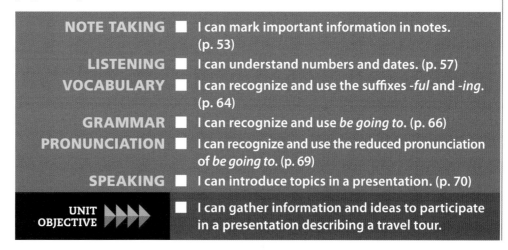

NOTE TAKING	☐	I can mark important information in notes. (p. 53)
LISTENING	☐	I can understand numbers and dates. (p. 57)
VOCABULARY	☐	I can recognize and use the suffixes -*ful* and -*ing*. (p. 64)
GRAMMAR	☐	I can recognize and use *be going to*. (p. 66)
PRONUNCIATION	☐	I can recognize and use the reduced pronunciation of *be going to*. (p. 69)
SPEAKING	☐	I can introduce topics in a presentation. (p. 70)
UNIT OBJECTIVE ▶▶▶▶	☐	I can gather information and ideas to participate in a presentation describing a travel tour.

LISTENING ▶ listening for specific information
NOTE TAKING ▶ making notes using a word web
VOCABULARY ▶ synonyms
GRAMMAR ▶ simple present for informal narratives
PRONUNCIATION ▶ simple present third-person -*s* / -*es*
SPEAKING ▶ using eye contact, tone of voice, and pause

UNIT QUESTION

Who makes you laugh?

A Discuss these questions with your classmates.

1. What funny TV shows do you like?

2. Do you tell jokes or make other people laugh?

3. Look at the photo. What are these people doing?

B Listen to *The Q Classroom* online. Then answer these questions.

1. What types of comedy or comedians do the students talk about?

2. Have you ever seen live comedy? If so, describe it.

3. Do you watch TV shows from another culture or in English or another language? Explain why you think they are funny or not funny.

 C Go to the Online Discussion Board to discuss the Unit Question with your classmates.

UNIT
OBJECTIVE ▶▶▶▶ Listen to a radio show and a lecture. Gather information
and ideas to tell a joke or a funny story.

75

D Look at the photo. The group is laughing at something they see on the laptop. What are possible reasons they are laughing? Write your ideas. Then discuss them with a partner.

_____

_____

_____

_____

A: I think they are laughing at a new YouTube video.

B: I think they are looking at someone's childhood pictures.

E Look at the chart. Write your answers. Then, with your partner, take turns asking for and giving information from the chart. Write your partner's answers in the chart.

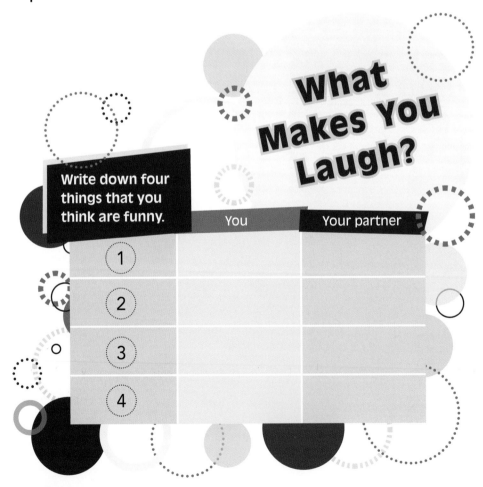

What Makes You Laugh?

Write down four things that you think are funny.	You	Your partner
1		
2		
3		
4		

LISTENING 1 | ## Charles Dickens—Making Readers Laugh After 200 Years

 **UNIT OBJECTIVE** ▶▶▶

You are going to listen to a radio show about the famous British author Charles Dickens. As you listen to the program, gather information and ideas about who makes you laugh.

PREVIEW THE LISTENING

A. **VOCABULARY** Here are some words from Listening 1. Read the sentences. Then write each <u>underlined</u> word next to the correct definition.

1. Mark Twain wrote <u>comical</u> stories, such as *Tom Sawyer* and *Huckleberry Finn*.

2. I think John will write a book someday. He is a very <u>talented</u> writer.

3. My boss has a great <u>sense of humor</u>. She makes everyone laugh.

4. Angelina is taking a writing course. She wants to be a <u>professional</u> writer someday.

5. That TV show was popular in the United States. <u>However</u>, it was not successful in other parts of the world.

6. That new TV show is a big <u>hit</u>. Lots of people watch it.

7. Kim told me a great story. She can <u>describe</u> things in a very funny way.

8. The Smiths' new house is <u>huge</u>. It has ten bedrooms!

a. _____ (*noun*) the ability to laugh at things and think they are funny

b. _____ (*adverb*) but

c. _____ (*adjective*) very big

d. _____ (*adjective*) doing something for money as a job

e. _____ (*adjective*) funny

f. _____ (*adjective*) able to do something well

g. _____ (*noun*) a person or thing that a lot of people like

h. _____ (*verb*) to explain

B. Go online for more practice with the vocabulary.

C. PREVIEW You are going to listen to a radio show about British writer Charles Dickens. What do you think makes Dickens's books funny?

The Old Curiosity Shop

Great Expectations

WORK WITH THE LISTENING

A. LISTEN AND TAKE NOTES Listen and number the topics in the order the speaker talks about them. There are two topics you will not use.

Tip for Success

Photos can help you predict the topic and main ideas of a listening.

_____ a. schooling

_____

_____ b. family

_____

_____ c. first professional writing job

_____

_____ d. university

_____

_____ e. characters

_____

_____ f. birthplace

_____

B. Listen again. On the lines in Activity A, write key words and phrases about the topics.

C. Circle the answer that best completes each statement.

1. People think Dickens's books are funny because ___.
   a. the stories and people are unusual
   b. Dickens's style of writing is old
   c. they are about funny events in history

2. Many of Dickens's characters ___.
   a. have the same names as his family members
   b. are similar to real people
   c. are from the southeast part of England

3. Dickens learned to be a writer ___.
   a. when he attended college
   b. because he had a difficult life growing up
   c. working for *Pickwick Papers Magazine*

4. Dickens's stories are often about the lives of ___.
   a. sad people
   b. poor people
   c. comical people

5. Dickens was very good at ___.
   a. having interesting conversations
   b. telling very sad stories
   c. making characters seem real

D. Circle the correct information to complete each sentence.

1. As a young boy, Dickens spent a lot of time (playing with friends outdoors / traveling around the country / reading).

2. Dickens had to leave school because he did not have enough (time / money / talent).

3. When Dickens was a boy, he had to work in a shoe polish factory because (he wanted to save a lot of money / his father had money problems / he wanted to publish his books).

4. Dickens's first novel was (not very popular / a big success / only sold in London).

E. Use words from the box to complete the sentences that explain why people think Dickens's books are funny.

comical	conversations	describes	humor	unusual

1. The characters are _____ and have _____ names.

2. Dickens _____ each character so well, you feel like you know them personally.

3. The _____ between the characters are often very funny.

4. Dickens helps us see _____ in the sad parts of life.

SAY WHAT YOU THINK

Discuss the questions in a group.

1. Why do people think Charles Dickens's books are comical? Do you think this type of humor is funny?

2. Do you like to read comical books or novels? What kind of stories do you think are funny?

3. Who are famous funny people from your country? Why do you think they are popular?

Listening Skill	Listening for specific information

Listening for specific information means listening for the important details you need. We listen for specific information especially when we listen to news or weather reports, transportation schedules, and instructions.

Specific information includes details such as these.

- names of people or places
- numbers, dates, or times (See the Unit 3 Listening Skill, page 57.)
- events

A. Read the information below. Then listen to Listening 1 again and write the missing information.

1. How many novels Charles Dickens wrote: _____

2. When Charles Dickens was born: _____

3. When his family moved to Kent in southeast England: _____

4. Where he got his first professional writing job:

   _____

5. How old he was when he stopped going to school: _____

B. Listen to the information about Charles Dickens. Write the missing information.

Tip for Success

Many radio stations put their radio shows on their websites. You can listen to them as many times as you like. This is a great way to practice listening.

Unlike some authors who only have one or two hits, _____ of

₁

Dickens's 15 books became very famous. One of his most popular works

is *David Copperfield*. *David Copperfield* was Dickens's _____ novel,

₂

which he wrote in _____. In the book, the main character, _____,

₃   ₄

tells the story of his own life. Like Dickens, David has a difficult life when

he is young. His parents die when he is a boy, and he must go to work in a

_____. Many parts of the story are sad. But as always, the way Dickens

₅

describes his characters makes readers laugh. In the end, David becomes a

successful _____, and lives a happy life. Late in his career, Dickens said

₆

that David Copperfield was his favorite of all of the characters in his books.

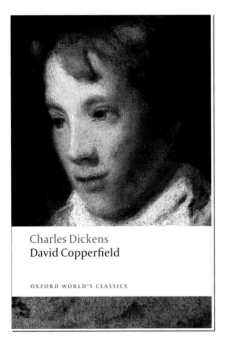

Charles Dickens
David Copperfield

OXFORD WORLD'S CLASSICS

C. Go online for more practice with listening for specific information.

Before you speak in class, in a discussion, or for a presentation, it is useful to take time to gather some ideas about what you want to say. This will help you remember the vocabulary you need and share your ideas more clearly. A **word web** is a good way to gather your ideas.

Look at a student's word web for the question "What makes you laugh?"

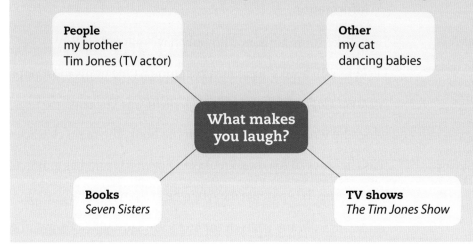

A. Complete the word web below for the Unit Question, "Who makes you laugh?"

B. Compare word webs with a partner.

 C. Go online for more practice with making notes using a word web.

 **UNIT OBJECTIVE** ▶▶▶▶ You are going to listen to a guest speaker in a university lecture. In the lecture, he talks with the professor about people's sense of humor. As you listen to the lecture, gather information and ideas about who makes you laugh.

PREVIEW THE LISTENING

A. **VOCABULARY** Here are some words and phrases from Listening 2. Read the sentences. Circle the answer that best matches the meaning of each <u>underlined</u> word or phrase.

1. Sometimes it's difficult to <u>communicate</u> in another language.
   a. to talk to people
   b. to look at people

2. Do you think it's funny to <u>make fun of</u> other people?
   a. to talk quietly to
   b. to laugh at in an unkind way

3. Oh, no! I brought the <u>wrong</u> book to English class. This is my Spanish book.
   a. incorrect
   b. interesting

Vocabulary Skill Review

In Unit 3, you learned about the suffixes *-ful* and *-ing*. Look at the word *interesting* in item 3. How can you change this word into a verb?

4. Some people don't like to show their <u>feelings</u>. They don't laugh or cry in front of other people.
   a. emotions such as happiness and anger
   b. parts of the body

5. Sometimes I don't <u>understand</u> jokes in English. I feel confused about what is funny.
   a. to know what something means
   b. to listen carefully to

6. Rei has a great sense of humor. She will <u>probably</u> laugh when I tell her the joke.
   a. not really
   b. almost certainly

7. Marisol is <u>afraid</u> to stand in front of an audience. She feels very nervous.
   a. scared
   b. happy

8. Close your eyes and <u>imagine</u> that you are at the beach.
   a. to make a picture in your mind
   b. to draw a picture on paper

 B. Go online for more practice with the vocabulary.

C. **PREVIEW** You are going to listen to a university lecture about different people's sense of humor. What is your sense of humor? Check (✓) the things that make you laugh. Then compare answers with your classmates.

- ☐ playing with babies / small children
- ☐ seeing cute animals
- ☐ other people falling down
- ☐ someone telling a joke
- ☐ watching comedy TV shows / cartoons
- ☐ reading humorous books
- ☐ making a mistake / doing something embarrassing
- ☐ other: _____

WORK WITH THE LISTENING

A. **LISTEN AND TAKE NOTES** Listen to the presentation and complete the student's word web with definitions of the four types of humor the presenter talks about.

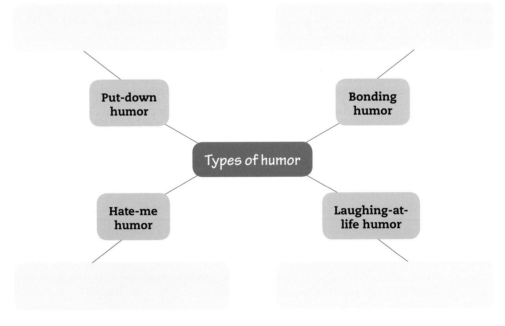

B. Compare word webs with a partner. Add one more box to each type of sense of humor in your word web. Then listen again and add one example for each sense of humor.

C. Read the items. Circle the answer that best describes each type of humor.

1. Put-down humor ___.
   a. helps us feel relaxed
   b. is the most common style
   c. makes fun of others

2. Bonding humor ___.
   a. is not very nice
   b. brings people together
   c. makes other people feel afraid

3. Hate-me humor makes fun of ___.
   a. people you dislike
   b. silly things
   c. yourself

4. Laughing-at-life humor ___.
   a. makes life easier
   b. is difficult to understand
   c. makes other people sad

D. Read the statements. Write *T* (true) or *F* (false). Then correct any false statements.

___ 1. Doctor Long feels that a sense of humor shows we are happy.

_____

___ 2. He thinks put-down humor is a way to make friends.

_____

___ 3. He says that people who use bonding humor like to tell jokes.

_____

___ 4. Hate-me humor does not mean we want people to dislike us.

_____

___ 5. Doctor Long says people who have the laughing-at-life humor style often have a sad life.

_____

E. Complete each sentence with your own words. Then compare answers with a partner.

1. Dr. Long says that humor helps us _____.

2. Humor is also one way that people _____.

3. Sometimes put-down humor can make people feel _____.

4. People who use bonding humor are _____

_____.

5. When people use hate-me humor, they _____.

6. People with the laughing-at-life humor style _____.

F. Read these examples of the four humor styles. Which styles are they? Write *put-down*, *bonding*, *hate-me*, or *laughing-at-life*.

_____ 1. A student often says he is not smart, is a bad student, etc., to make other students laugh at him.

_____ 2. A student gets a bad grade on a test. Another student says, "Congratulations! You got the lowest score!"

_____ 3. A student gets a bad grade on the test. She laughs and says, "I should study more next time."

_____ 4. A student likes to be in the center of a group, telling funny stories and jokes.

 **G.** Go online to listen to *Humor in Classic Literature* and check your comprehension.

 SAY WHAT YOU THINK

A. Discuss the questions in a group.

1. Do you agree that it's very important for a person to have a sense of humor? Why or why not?

2. Do you know any people with one of the four main humor types? Who are they? Describe them. What do they say or do?

3. Which style is most like your sense of humor? Why do you think so?

B. Before you watch the video, discuss the questions in a group.

When we communicate with other people, what are some examples of ways we show that we think something is funny . . .

- in person?
- in writing?
- on a computer or smartphone?

C. Go online to watch the video about the science of smiling. Then check your comprehension.

emotion *(n.)* a feeling

facial expression *(n.)* the way the face moves to show the way we feel

identify *(v.)* to understand

sophisticated *(adj.)* advanced and complicated

D. Think about the unit video, Listening 1, and Listening 2 as you discuss the questions.

1. Do you like to laugh at yourself? Why or why not?

2. How is humor different in different situations, for example, in person, on the phone, in writing, or on the computer?

Vocabulary Skill Synonyms

Synonyms are words that have almost the same or a similar meaning. The dictionary often gives synonyms in the definition of a word. In the example, a synonym is given for *funny*.

---

fun·ny 🔑 /ˈfʌni/ *adjective* (fun·ni·er, fun·ni·est)
1 making you laugh or smile: *a funny story* •
He's so funny! ➔ **SYNONYM amusing**
2 strange or surprising: *There's a funny smell in this room.*

You can build your vocabulary by learning synonyms for words you already know. Learning synonyms will help you understand more when you listen.

A. Read the sentences. Write a synonym from the box for each <u>underlined</u> word or phrase. You may use some synonyms more than once. Use your dictionary to help you.

famous	funny	huge	laugh	feelings

1. Did you read the book *James and the Giant Peach*? It's about an <u>enormous</u> peach.

   enormous: _____

2. My friend Tomás is <u>hilarious</u>. He always makes me laugh.

   hilarious: _____

3. Charles Dickens started writing when he was a young boy. But he didn't become <u>well known</u> until he published his first novel.

   well known: _____

4. Poets often write about different <u>emotions</u> such as anger or excitement.

   emotions: _____

5. Those two students are rude. They sit in the back of the class and <u>giggle</u>.

   giggle: _____

6. Children often make <u>silly</u> faces to make other kids laugh.

   silly: _____

B. Look in the dictionary to find one more synonym for each word. Write a sentence with each new synonym.

1. Word: huge   Synonym: _____

   Sentence: _____

2. Word: laugh   Synonym: _____

   Sentence: _____

3. Word: funny   Synonym: _____

   Sentence: _____

C. Read your synonyms and sentences from Activity B to a partner.

iQ ONLINE   **D.** Go online for more practice with synonyms.

SPEAKING

UNIT OBJECTIVE ▶▶▶▶ At the end of this unit, you are going to tell a joke or funny story to a group (or to the class). As you tell your joke or story, you will need to use appropriate eye contact, tone of voice, and pause.

Grammar | **Simple present for informal narratives**

When you tell a short, informal narrative, like a story or a joke, you can use the simple present even if the story happened in the past.

> A man **walks** into a shop and **sees** a little rabbit. He **asks** the shopkeeper, "Does your rabbit bite?"
> The shopkeeper **says**, "No, my rabbit doesn't bite."
> The man **touches** the rabbit, and the rabbit **bites** him.
> "Ouch!" he **says**. "You said your rabbit doesn't bite!"
> The shopkeeper **replies**, "That isn't my rabbit!"

A. Complete these jokes with the simple present form of the verbs in the box. Then listen and check your answers.

1. | bring | go | order | reply | say |

   A man and a woman _____ to a restaurant
      1
   for lunch. The woman _____ a bowl of soup.
                                    2
   A few minutes later, the waiter _____ the soup
                                                3
   to the table. The man _____, "Excuse me. Your finger
                                      4
   is in my wife's soup." The waiter _____, "Oh, that's OK.
                                                  5
   It isn't too hot."

2. | answer | ask | be | say | think |

   A man _____ at the doctor's office.
                1
   The doctor _____ him, "What's the trouble?"
                          2
   The man _____, "I hurt everywhere. It hurts when
                      3
   I touch my head. It hurts when I touch my leg, and it hurts when

▶▶▶▶ | Listening and Speaking   **89**

I touch my arm." The doctor _____ for a moment.
                                        4

Then he _____, "I know what's wrong. Your finger
                  5

is broken!"

3.
| ask | look | say | see | stop | tell |

A man _____ his car at a traffic light.
                        1

A policeman stops next to him and _____ a penguin
                                                      2

in the car. The policeman _____ the man, "You can't
                                    3

drive with a penguin in your car. Take that penguin to the zoo."

The man _____, "Yes, sir. I will." The next day, the
                    4

policeman sees the man's car again. The penguin is still in the car.

The policeman _____, "Why do you have that penguin?
                        5

I told you to take it to the zoo!" The man _____ at the
                                                          6

policeman and says, "I did that yesterday, and we had a great time!

Today we're going to the park!"

Critical Thinking Tip

In Activity B, you learn a joke and tell it. **Restating**, or saying something again in your own words, is a good way to share information.

B. Work in a group. Choose a joke from Activity A. Study the joke and try to remember it. You can write some notes below to help you. Take turns telling the jokes using the simple present. Look at your classmates; don't read from your book.

_____

_____

_____

C. Go online for more practice using the simple present for informal narratives.

D. Go online for the grammar expansion.

The **simple present third-person singular** form of a regular verb ends in either -*s* or -*es*.

> He eats a lot.
> She washes her hands.

The pronunciation of this final sound depends on the sound at the end of the base verb. There are three possible sounds:

- The -*s* = /z/ when the sound is **voiced** (with sound). This includes all vowel sounds, and the consonants: /b/, /d/, /g/, /l/, /m/, /n/, /ŋ/ (ri**ng**), /r/, /ð/ (brea**th**, fa**th**er), and /v/.
- The -*s* = /s/ when the sound is **unvoiced** (without sound), including /f/, /k/, /p/, and /t/.
- The -*s*/-*es* = /əz/ when the final sound is an -*s* or -*z* like sound, including /dʒ/ (ju**dg**e), /s/, /ʃ/ (wi**sh**), /tʃ/ (wa**tch**), and /z/.

Read and listen to the examples in the chart.

If the base verb ends in . . .	Base verb	*he / she / it*
a voiced sound, pronounce the third-person singular with /z/.	say	says
	tell	tells
	give	gives
	answer	answers
an unvoiced sound, pronounce the third-person singular with /s/.	laugh	laughs
	look	looks
	stop	stops
	eat	eats
an -*s* or -*z* like sound, pronounce the third-person singular with /əz/.	change	changes
	miss	misses
	wash	washes
	watch	watches

A. Read each joke and <u>underline</u> every simple present third-person verb ending in *-s* or *-es*. Write /z/, /s/, or /əz/ above each *-s* or *-es* to indicate the pronunciation.

1. **In the shop**

   A man walks into a shop and sees a little rabbit. He asks the

   shopkeeper, "Does your rabbit bite?"

   The shopkeeper says, "No, my rabbit doesn't bite."

   The man touches the rabbit, and the rabbit bites him.

   "Ouch!" he says. "You said your rabbit doesn't bite!"

   The shopkeeper replies, "That isn't my rabbit!"

Tip for Success

You can use the simple present third-person *-s* and *-es* pronunciation rules for the pronunciation of plural forms, too. For example, the plural of *boot* is *boots*. The *-s* is an unvoiced /s/ sound.

2. **At school**

   A five-year-old boy asks his teacher to help him put on his boots.

   The teacher says, "Of course," and he starts to help the boy. He pushes

   and pulls on the boots, but they don't go on the boy's feet. He gets very

   tired, so he takes a rest.

   The little boy says, "Teacher, these aren't my boots."

   "Why didn't you tell me?" the teacher asks.

   The boy replies, "They're my brother's boots. My mom made me wear

   them today."

   The teacher pushes and pulls on the boots some more, and finally,

   he gets them on the boy's feet.

   "OK! Now, where are your gloves?" he asks the boy.

   The boy answers, "I put them in my boots!"

B. Work with a partner. Take turns reading the jokes aloud. Use the correct pronunciation of the third-person singular endings.

C. Go online for more practice with simple present third-person *-s* / *-es*.

When you tell a story or a joke, there are different ways to make it more interesting.

- **Make eye contact with the listener(s).** This will help you connect with your audience and keep them interested.
- **Use your voice to express different feelings.** This helps the listener(s) understand the feelings of the people in the story.
- **Pause—stop speaking for a moment**—before you say the punch line (the end of a story or joke). This can help to make the ending a surprise.

Listen to the example.

The man touches the rabbit, and the rabbit bites him.
"Ouch!" he says. "You said your rabbit doesn't bite!"
<u>   </u>   <u>   </u>
surprised/angry tone of voice

The shopkeeper replies, "That isn't my rabbit!"
↑
pause

A. Listen to the joke. <u>Underline</u> the places where the speaker uses tone of voice. Draw an arrow (↑) where the speaker pauses.

A man is at the doctor's office. The doctor asks him, "What's the trouble?" The man answers, "I hurt everywhere. It hurts when I touch my head. It hurts when I touch my leg, and it hurts when I touch my arm." The doctor thinks for a moment. Then he says, "I know what's wrong. Your finger is broken!"

B. Work with a partner. Read the joke in Activity A aloud. Practice making eye contact, using tone of voice, and pausing.

C. Read these excerpts from jokes. <u>Underline</u> the places where you can use tone of voice. Draw an arrow (↑) where you can pause.

1. A few minutes later, the waiter brings the soup to the table. The man says, "Excuse me. Your finger is in my wife's soup." The waiter replies, "Oh, that's OK. It isn't too hot."

2. The next day, the policeman sees the man's car again. The penguin is still in the car. The policeman asks, "Why do you have that penguin? I told you to take it to the zoo!" The man looks at the policeman and says, "I did that yesterday, and we had a great time! Today we're going to the park!"

D. Work in a group. Take turns reading aloud the excerpts in Activity C. Remember to make eye contact, use tone of voice, and pause before the end.

 E. Go online for more practice with using eye contact, tone of voice, and pause.

Unit Assignment | Tell a joke or a funny story

 In this assignment, you are going to tell a joke or funny story to a group (or to the class). As you prepare your joke or story, think about the Unit Question, "Who makes you laugh?" Use information from Listening 1, Listening 2, the unit video, and your work in the unit to support your joke or story. Refer to the Self-Assessment checklist on page 96.

CONSIDER THE IDEAS

A. Read the joke and try to guess the punch line (the last line).

A tourist visits Sydney, Australia. He wants to go to the beach. But he doesn't know how to get there. He sees a policeman. He waves to the policeman and says, "Excuse me! Can you help me?"

The policeman comes over and says, "Yes, sir. How can I help you?"

The tourist says, "Can you tell me the fastest way to get to the beach?"

The policeman asks, "Are you walking or driving?"

The tourist answers, "Driving."

The policeman answers, "_____."

B. Listen to an Australian comedian tell the joke in Activity A. Write the punch line in Activity A above.

C. Listen again and discuss these questions with a partner.

1. Do you understand the joke?

2. Do you think the comedian was good? Why or why not?

3. Where in the joke did the comedian use tone of voice or pause? Underline where his tone of voice changed and draw an arrow (↑) where there was a pause.

PREPARE AND SPEAK

A. **GATHER IDEAS** Think of a joke or a funny story you want to tell. It can be a joke or story you know or a story about something that happened to you or someone you know. Use a word web to make notes and gather ideas for your joke or story.

B. **ORGANIZE IDEAS** Make notes about your joke or story. Remember that you can use the simple present. Then complete the tasks below.

1. Underline places in your joke or story where you can use tone of voice. Draw an arrow (↑) in the place where you can pause (before the punch line).

2. Practice telling your joke or funny story to a partner. Use eye contact, tone of voice, and a pause to make the joke more interesting.

C. **SPEAK** Tell your joke or story to a group (or to the class). Refer to the Self-Assessment checklist on page 96 before you begin.

 Go online for your alternate Unit Assignment.

CHECK AND REFLECT

A. CHECK Think about the Unit Assignment as you complete the Self-Assessment checklist.

SELF-ASSESSMENT		
Yes	No	
☐	☐	I was able to speak easily about the topic.
☐	☐	I used a word web to gather ideas and take notes.
☐	☐	My partner/group/class understood me and thought I was funny.
☐	☐	I used the simple present to tell a joke/funny story.
☐	☐	I used vocabulary from the unit.
☐	☐	I used eye contact, tone of voice, and pause when telling a joke/funny story.
☐	☐	I pronounced the simple present third-person -s/-es correctly.

B. REFLECT Go to the Online Discussion Board to discuss these questions.

1. What is something new you learned in this unit?

2. Look back at the Unit Question—Who makes you laugh? Is your answer different now than when you started the unit? If yes, how is it different? Why?

TRACK YOUR SUCCESS

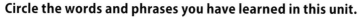

Circle the words and phrases you have learned in this unit.

Nouns
feelings 🔑
hit 🔑

Verbs
communicate 🔑 AWL
describe 🔑
imagine 🔑
understand 🔑

Adjectives
afraid 🔑
comical
funny 🔑
huge 🔑
professional 🔑 AWL
talented
wrong 🔑

Adverbs
however 🔑
probably 🔑

Phrases
make fun of
sense of humor

🔑 Oxford 2000 keywords
AWL Academic Word List

Check (✓) the skills you learned. If you need more work on a skill, refer to the page(s) in parentheses.

LISTENING	☐ I can listen for specific information. (p. 80)
NOTE TAKING	☐ I can use a word web to make notes and gather ideas. (p. 82)
VOCABULARY	☐ I can recognize and use synonyms. (p. 87)
GRAMMAR	☐ I can recognize and use the simple present for informal narratives. (p. 89)
PRONUNCIATION	☐ I can recognize and pronounce the simple present third-person *-s/-es*. (p. 91)
SPEAKING	☐ I can use eye contact, tone of voice, and pause. (p. 93)
UNIT OBJECTIVE ▶▶▶▶	☐ I can gather information and ideas to tell a joke or a funny story.

AUTHORS AND CONSULTANTS

Author

Jaimie Scanlon is a freelance ELT materials writer/editor and teacher trainer. She holds a Master's degree in TESOL and French from the School for International Training, where she concentrated on language pedagogy, applied linguistics, and curriculum design. Over the past 20 years, she has taught English language learners of all ages and has trained teachers in Asia, Eastern Europe, and the U.S. She lives in southern Vermont with her husband and two children.

Series Consultants

ONLINE INTEGRATION

Chantal Hemmi holds an Ed.D. TEFL and is a Japan-based teacher trainer and curriculum designer. Since leaving her position as Academic Director of the British Council in Tokyo, she has been teaching at the Center for Language Education and Research at Sophia University on an EAP/CLIL program offered for undergraduates. She delivers lectures and teacher trainings throughout Japan, Indonesia, and Malaysia.

COMMUNICATIVE GRAMMAR

Nancy Schoenfeld holds an M.A. in TESOL from Biola University in La Mirada, California, and has been an English language instructor since 2000. She has taught ESL in California and Hawaii, and EFL in Thailand and Kuwait. She has also trained teachers in the United States and Indonesia. Her interests include teaching vocabulary, extensive reading, and student motivation. She is currently an English Language Instructor at Kuwait University.

WRITING

Marguerite Ann Snow holds a Ph.D. in Applied Linguistics from UCLA. She teaches in the TESOL M.A. program in the Charter College of Education at California State University, Los Angeles. She was a Fulbright scholar in Hong Kong and Cyprus. In 2006, she received the President's Distinguished Professor award at Cal State, LA. She has trained EFL teachers in Algeria, Argentina, Brazil, Egypt, Libya, Morocco, Pakistan, Peru, Spain, and Turkey. She is the author/editor of publications in the areas of integrated content, English for academic purposes, and standards for English teaching and learning. She recently served as a co-editor of *Teaching English as a Second or Foreign Language* (4th ed.).

VOCABULARY

Cheryl Boyd Zimmerman is a Professor at California State University, Fullerton. She specializes in second-language vocabulary acquisition, an area in which she is widely published. She teaches graduate courses on second-language acquisition, culture, vocabulary, and the fundamentals of TESOL and is a frequent invited speaker on topics related to vocabulary teaching and learning. She is the author of *Word Knowledge: A Vocabulary Teacher's Handbook* and Series Director of *Inside Reading, Inside Writing,* and *Inside Listening and Speaking,* all published by Oxford University Press.

ASSESSMENT

Lawrence J. Zwier holds an M.A. in TESL from the University of Minnesota. He is currently the Associate Director for Curriculum Development at the English Language Center at Michigan State University in East Lansing. He has taught ESL/EFL in the United States, Saudi Arabia, Malaysia, Japan, and Singapore.

AUDIO TRACK LIST

Audio can be found in the *iQ Online* Media Center. Go to iQOnlinePractice.com. Click on the Media Center . Choose to stream or download ⬇ the audio file you select. Not all audio files are available for download.

Page	Track Name: Q2e_01_LS_
2	U01_Q_Classroom.mp3
5	U01_NoteTakingSkill_ActivityA.mp3
7	U01_Listening1_ActivityA.mp3
7	U01_Listening1_ActivityB.mp3
8	U01_Listening1_ActivityF.mp3
9	U01_ListeningSkill_Example.mp3
9	U01_ListeningSkill_ActivityA.mp3
10	U01_ListeningSkill_ActivityB.mp3
11	U01_Listening2_ActivityA.mp3
11	U01_Listening2_ActivityB.mp3
12	U01_Listening2_ActivityC.mp3
19	U01_Pronunciation_Examples.mp3
20	U01_Pronunciation_ActivityB.mp3
21	U01_SpeakingSkill_ActivityA.mp3
21	U01_SpeakingSkill_ActivityB.mp3
27	U02_Q_Classroom.mp3
29	U02_NoteTakingSkill_ActivityA.mp3
31	U02_Listening1_ActivityA.mp3
31	U02_Listening1_ActivityB.mp3
34	U02_ListeningSkill_ActivityA.mp3
34	U02_ListeningSkill_ActivityB.mp3
36	U02_Listening2_ActivityA.mp3
36	U02_Listening2_ActivityC.mp3
40	U02_VocabularySkill_ActivityA.mp3
40	U02_VocabularySkill_ActivityB.mp3
41	U02_Grammar_Part1_ActivityA.mp3
42	U02_Grammar_Part2_ActivityA.mp3
43	U02_Pronunciation_Examples.mp3
44	U02_Pronunciation_ActivityA.mp3
51	U03_Q_Classroom.mp3
53	U03_NoteTakingSkill_Example.mp3
53	U03_NoteTakingSkill_ActivityA.mp3
55	U03_Listening1_ActivityA.mp3
55	U03_Listening1_ActivityC.mp3
56	U03_Listening1_ActivityE.mp3
57	U03_ListeningSkill_Example1.mp3
57	U03_ListeningSkill_Example2.mp3
57	U03_ListeningSkill_Example3.mp3
58	U03_ListeningSkill_ActivityA.mp3
59	U03_ListeningSkill_ActivityC.mp3
61	U03_Listening2_ActivityA.mp3
62	U03_Listening2_ActivityB.mp3
68	U03_Grammar_ActivityB.mp3
69	U03_Pronunciation_Examples.mp3
71	U03_UnitAssignment_ActivityA.mp3
71	U03_UnitAssignment_ActivityB.mp3

Page	Track Name: Q2e_01_LS_
74	U04_Q_Classroom.mp3
78	U04_Listening1_ActivityA.mp3
79	U04_Listening1_ActivityB.mp3
80	U04_ListeningSkill_ActivityA.mp3
81	U04_ListeningSkill_ActivityB.mp3
84	U04_Listening2_ActivityA.mp3
84	U04_Listening2_ActivityB.mp3
89	U04_Grammar_ActivityA.mp3
91	U04_Pronunciation_Examples.mp3
93	U04_SpeakingSkill_Example.mp3
93	U04_SpeakingSkill_ActivityA.mp3
95	U04_UnitAssignment_ActivityB.mp3
95	U04_UnitAssignment_ActivityC.mp3
99	U05_Q_Classroom.mp3
101	U05_NoteTakingSkill_Example.mp3
101	U05_NoteTakingSkill_ActivityA.mp3
103	U05_Listening1_ActivityA.mp3
103	U05_Listening1_ActivityC.mp3
105	U05_ListeningSkill_ActivityA.mp3
107	U05_Listening2_ActivityA.mp3
108	U05_Listening2_ActivityC.mp3
112	U05_Grammar_ActivityA.mp3
114	U05_Pronunciation_Example1.mp3
114	U05_Pronunciation_Example2.mp3
114	U05_Pronunciation_Example3.mp3
115	U05_Pronunciation_ActivityB.mp3
116	U05_UnitAssignment.mp3
120	U06_Q_Classroom.mp3
123	U06_NoteTakingSkill_Example.mp3
123	U06_NoteTakingSkill_ActivityA.mp3
125	U06_Listening1_ActivityA.mp3
126	U06_Listening1_ActivityC.mp3
128	U06_ListeningSkill_ActivityA.mp3
128	U06_ListeningSkill_ActivityB.mp3
130	U06_Listening2_ActivityA.mp3
131	U06_Listening2_ActivityE.mp3
133	U06_VocabularySkill_ActivityA.mp3
136	U06_Pronunciation_Examples.mp3
137	U06_Pronunciation_ActivityA.mp3
138	U06_SpeakingSkill_ActivityA.mp3
139	U06_UnitAssignment.mp3

Page	Track Name: Q2e_01_LS_
142	U07_Q_Classroom.mp3
147	U07_Listening1_ActivityA.mp3
147	U07_Listening1_ActivityC.mp3
149	U07_ListeningSkill_ActivityA.mp3
152	U07_Listening2_ActivityA.mp3
152	U07_Listening2_ActivityB.mp3
155	U07_VocabularySkill_ActivityA.mp3
159	U07_Pronunciation_Examples.mp3
159	U07_Pronunciation_ActivityA.mp3
159	U07_Pronunciation_ActivityB.mp3
160	U07_NoteTakingSkill_Example.mp3
161	U07_NoteTakingSkill_ActivityA.mp3
162	U07_UnitAssignment.mp3
167	U08_Q_Classroom.mp3
172	U08_Listening1_ActivityA.mp3
173	U08_Listening1_ActivityB.mp3
175	U08_ListeningSkill_ActivityA.mp3
177	U08_Listening2_ActivityA.mp3
177	U08_Listening2_ActivityB.mp3
182	U08_Pronunciation_Example1.mp3
182	U08_Pronunciation_Example2.mp3
183	U08_Pronunciation_ActivityB.mp3
185	U08_UnitAssignment.mp3

OXFORD
UNIVERSITY PRESS

198 Madison Avenue
New York, NY 10016 USA

Great Clarendon Street, Oxford, OX2 6DP, United Kingdom

Oxford University Press is a department of the University of Oxford.
It furthers the University's objective of excellence in research, scholarship,
and education by publishing worldwide. Oxford is a registered trade
mark of Oxford University Press in the UK and in certain other countries

Director, ELT New York: Laura Pearson
Head of Adult, ELT New York: Stephanie Karras
Publisher: Sharon Sargent
Managing Editor: Mariel DeKranis
Development Editor: Eric Zuarino
Executive Art and Design Manager: Maj-Britt Hagsted
Design Project Manager: Debbie Lofaso
Content Production Manager: Julie Armstrong
Senior Production Artist: Elissa Santos
Image Manager: Trisha Masterson
Image Editor: Liaht Ziskind
Production Coordinator: Brad Tucker

ISBN: 978 0 19 481846 9 Student Book 1A with iQ Online pack
ISBN: 978 0 19 481847 6 Student Book 1A as pack component
ISBN: 978 0 19 481802 5 iQ Online student website

ACKNOWLEDGEMENTS

Illustrations by: p. 4 Barb Bastian; p. 22 Barb Bastian; p. 28 Barb Bastian; p. 56
5W Infographics; p. 76 Bill Smith Group; p. 100 Barb Bastian; p. 103 Jean
Tuttle; p. 144 Greg Paprocki; p. 158 Barb Bastian; p. 168 Barb Bastian; p. 182
Jean Tuttle

*We would also like to thank the following for permission to reproduce the following
photographs:* Cover: David Pu'u/Corbis; Video Vocabulary (used throughout
the book): Oleksiy Mark / Shutterstock; p. 2/3 JONATHAN ALCORN/Corbis
UK Ltd.; p. 4 Blend Images/Alamy (office); p. 4 Image Source/Getty Images
(waiter); p. 4 Juice Images/Getty Images (store); p. 4 Steve Hix/Somos
Images/Corbis UK Ltd. (teacher); p. 6 Blend Images/Alamy; p. 18 PhotoAlto/
Oxford University Press; p. 26 Yaacov Dagan/Alamy; p. 26/27 George H.H.
Huey/Alamy; p. 27 laurentiu iordache/Alamy (masks); p. 27 Gianni Dagli
Orti/Corbis UK Ltd. (aztec); p. 36 Manfred Rutz/Getty Images (greeting);
p. 36 Chad Ehlers/Alamy (reading); p. 36 Stock Connection Distribution/
Alamy (flowers); p. 36 amana images inc./Alamy (card); p. 40 Photodisc/
Oxford University Press; p. 45 Julie Armstrong/Oxford University Press
(sphinx); p. 45 Julie Armstrong/Oxford University Press (flowers); p. 45
Julie Armstrong/Oxford University Press (Rocks); p. 50 Kameleon007 /
iStockphoto (instruments); p. 50 epa european pressphoto agency b.v./
Alamy (balloons); p. 51 eye35 stock/Alamy (keyring); p. 51 Africa Studio/
Shutterstock (suitcase); p. 52 Nataliya Popova/Shutterstock (no littering);
p. 52 RATOCA/Shutterstock (camera); p. 52 Arcady/Shutterstock (flowers);
p. 52 ValeStock/Shutterstock (bird); p. 52 Evgenia Bolyukh/Shutterstock
(fire); p. 52 Zanna Art/Shutterstock (grass); p. 55 Anna Yu/Alamy (bus); p. 55
Larry Lilac/Oxford University Press (wall); p. 55 imageBROKER/Alamy (boat);
p. 55 Frans Lanting Studio/Alamy (penguins); p. 59 Jon Arnold Images Ltd/
Alamy (eiffel); p. 59 Philipus/Alamy (buji); p. 59 Lonely Planet Images/Alamy
(waterfall); p. 59 Imagebroker/Alamy (mountains); p. 61 Paul Springett
08/Alamy (Machu Picchu); p. 61 Kiselev Andrey Valerevich/Shutterstock
(backpacker); p. 61 Bob Daemmrich/Alamy (teacher); p. 61 Adrian Sherratt/
Alamy (painting); p. 61 Milla Kontkanen/Alamy (beach); p. 65 Sarmu/Getty
Images; p. 67 John Harper/Corbis UK Ltd.; p. 74/75 Tom Merton/Getty
Images; p. 76 Mango Productions/Corbis UK Ltd.; p. 78 AF archive/Alamy
(Dickens); p. 78 Classic Image/Alamy (house); p. 78 19th era/Alamy (dinner);
p. 81 Oxford University Press; p. 85 Photodisc/Oxford University Press;
p. 98 ANDREW YATES / Stringer/Getty Images; p. 99 herreid /iStockphoto
(badminton); p. 99 tarasov/Shutterstock (sports gear); p. 100 Christophe
Simon/AFP/Getty Images (swimmer); p. 100 Hemera/Thinkstock (baseball);
p. 100 Polka Dot Images/Oxford University Press (cyclist); p. 100 Aspen
Photo/Shutterstock (basketball); p. 104 James Oliver/Oxford University Press
(track); p. 104 Photodisc/Oxford University Press (race); p. 107 Photodisc/
Oxford University Press (tennis); p. 107 Image Source/Oxford University
Press (training); p. 107 Jim West/Alamy (hockey); p. 107 Photodisc/Oxford
University Press (karate); p. 107 Photodisc/Oxford University Press (cycling);
p. 120/121 Spencer Grant / Art Directors/Alamy; p. 122 Nycretoucher/
Getty Images; p. 125 www.jupiterimages.com/Getty Images; p. 127
DreamPictures/Getty Images (woman); p. 127 Mint Images - Tim Robbins/
Getty Images (man); p. 128 RubberBall/Alamy; p. 130 CandyBox Images/
Shutterstock; p. 134 Erik Isakson/Getty Images; p. 142/143 Rana Faure/
Corbis UK Ltd.; p. 146 Photodisc/Oxford University Press; p. 150 PhotoAlto/
Laurence Mouton/Oxford University Press; p. 162 Matt Hess/Golden Pixels
Llc/Corbis UK Ltd.; p. 166 Stephen Frink/Getty Images; p. 166/167 wacpan/
Shutterstock; p. 167 2011 Gamma-Rapho/Getty Images (rollercoaster); p. 167
UNIVERSAL / THE KOBAL COLLECTION/Kobal Collection (birds); p. 168
James Gerholdt/Peter Arnold Images/Getty Images (snake); p. 168 PhotoAlto/
Alamy (elevator); p. 168 PhotosIndia.com/Getty Images (speaker); p. 168 Alex
Benwell/Alamy (skyscrapers); p. 168 Barry Mason/Alamy (airplane); p. 168
LorenRyePhoto/Alamy (lightning); p. 172 William Radcliffe/Science Faction/
Corbis UK Ltd.; p. 174 David Wall/Alamy; p. 176 James W. Porter/Corbis UK
Ltd.; p. 177 Kiichiro Sato/AP Photo/Press Association Images; p. 178 Pegaz/
Alamy; p. 185 Don Johnston/Getty Images.